CW01084021

Lean Supplier Development

Establishing Partnerships and True Costs Throughout the Supply Chain

Lean Supplier Development

Establishing Partnerships and True Costs Throughout the Supply Chain

Chris Harris • Rick Harris • Chuck Streeter

CRC Press
Taylor & Francis Group
Boca Raton   London   New York

CRC Press is an imprint of the
Taylor & Francis Group, an **informa** business

A PRODUCTIVITY PRESS BOOK

Productivity Press
Taylor & Francis Group
270 Madison Avenue
New York, NY 10016

Library of Congress Cataloging-in-Publication Data

Harris, Chris, 1976-
    Lean supplier development : establishing partnerships and true costs throughout the supply chain / Chris Harris, Rick Harris, and Chuck Streeter.
        p. cm.
    Includes bibliographical references and index.
    1. Cost control. 2. Industrial procurement--Cost control. 3. Business planning. I. Harris, Rick, 1953 Aug. 2- II. Streeter, Chuck. III. Title.

HD47.3.H36 2010
658.7'22--dc22   2010002405

Visit the Taylor & Francis Web site at
http://www.taylorandfrancis.com

and the Productivity Press Web site at
http://www.productivitypress.com

Contents

Preface

In 2005, our book *Making Materials Flow** won the Shingo Prize for excellence in manufacturing research. Since then, we've had the good fortune of helping a number of individuals and facilities implement the principles of *Making Materials Flow* and develop robust internal material movement systems, which have reduced inventories and increased efficiencies. On the heels of their success, many facilities are ready to take the next step: to develop their suppliers into long-term partners to support their internal material movement systems. In this book, we'll teach you how to increase your competitive edge by building those partnerships. But first, let's lay some groundwork, starting with a basic explanation of internal material movement systems and the mechanisms that comprise them.

When properly developed, a Lean internal material movement system will create the environment you need to effectively develop suppliers into partners, which can impact the entire value stream, from cash paid for raw materials to cash from the customer. An internal material movement system is a systematic approach for dealing with all material movement from the receiving door of the facility to the shipping door of the facility. Lean internal material movement systems are composed of four important parts: Plan for Every Part (PFEP), supermarket (purchased parts), pull signals (kanban), and route development (bus vs. taxi).

Plan For Every Part (PFEP)

The Plan for Every Part (PFEP) is a database vital to the effective implementation of both internal material movement and external material movement.

---

* Harris, R., C. Harris, and E. Wilson, Making Materials Flow—A Lean Material-Handling Guide for Operations, Production-Control, and Engineering Professionals (Cambridge, MA: The Lean Enterprise Institute, 2003).

The PFEP is the basis for good material movement because it contains information on all of your purchased components, work-in-process parts, and finished goods: all of the material in your facility. Think of it as the DNA of your facility.

You'll use the PFEP for multiple tasks: to calculate the appropriate inventory levels of purchased components, work-in-process components, and finished goods; and during the development of the internal material movement system as a tool to design, size, and implement the system. We'll go into this in more detail in later chapters, but for now, know that the PFEP is a vital database that you will create and use extensively as you develop your suppliers into partners.

The PFEP is foundational for supplier development because it gives us the information that we need to begin to work with suppliers. Because material normally makes up a large percentage of the cost of goods sold, you need a central database to hold important information on that material. As we've helped people implement Lean enterprise systems over the years, we have come to the conclusion that the PFEP, when used properly, is a central tool to effective and successful implementation.

Supermarket (Purchased Parts)

In a perfect world, the supplier of a purchased part would bring the part in and hand it to the production associate on an as-needed basis. We don't know about you, but we're not living in that perfect world. So, we need to find a way to effectively control the incoming material from suppliers. How? With the purchased parts supermarket.

A supermarket is an organized, sized, controlled, and monitored place where inventory is stored. It differs from a typical warehouse or storage point in that it serves a very specific purpose. Supermarkets serve as a buffer, whether between you and your supplier or from one process to the next. A well-designed and organized supermarket can help you facilitate effective material flow.

A supermarket with inventory that doesn't add value is waste, but it is sometimes necessary to effectively run a Lean enterprise system. The supermarket that we deal with first when we implement an internal material movement system is the purchased parts market. The purchased parts market is important because it is the base of operations. The purchased parts supermarket is the place where all purchased inventory is stored; in other words, every purchased component that comes into the facility goes into the purchased parts supermarket.

When a facility has a purchased parts supermarket, there is no guesswork regarding where the parts are stored. For example, have you ever expedited parts that your system indicated you already had in your facility? If you're like most people, chances are you've done just that. In a system where all purchased components are stored in one place, there is only one place that you have to look to see if you have the components. It's a far more efficient approach than having to go to the floor and look, or finding and asking a supervisor or the forklift truck driver if there are any parts in the various locations where they could be stored.

With a purchased parts supermarket, your facility can control its purchased parts to a degree that it's never been able to before. It also allows a total internal material movement system to be built. From a central purchased parts market, you can ensure effective and efficient delivery to the production floor as well as effective and efficient control of incoming material in the purchased parts supermarket. This is because all parts from suppliers must go into one central purchased parts supermarket, so you will know if someone has overshipped, undershipped, or shipped the wrong parts.

Note that one of the customers of a supplier development program is the purchased parts supermarket. Understanding the purchased parts supermarket and its role in the Lean enterprise is important to effectively developing suppliers into Lean partnerships.

Pull Signals (Kanban)

Pull signals are the next component of an effective internal material movement system. A pull signal represents information and authorization: information about the part number, where it is stored, where it is used, minimum levels, route, etc. Without proper information flow, there would be no knowledge of where the parts in the purchased parts supermarket should be delivered on the production floor. Pull signals come in different forms, but the most common is likely the kanban card.*

Pull signals are vital to the success of an internal material movement system. When an operator in the system gets ready to use the first part in a

---

* A kanban card is a pull signal, in the form of a card, that holds information on a standard pack of parts. It is used to signal that action needs to be taken with the corresponding material.

container of parts, the pull signal is pulled and given to the material delivery operator in an interval of time—unless it is a two-bin system, in which case the container is the signal and the signal does not get dropped until the last part in the container is used. This lets the material driver know that the parts are being used and that more parts are needed. The material delivery operator can now retrieve the needed parts from the purchased parts supermarket and deliver parts on his or her next route (explained in the next section) to the production associate. A Lean material movement system is based on replenishment, meaning, if you use parts, you will get more parts, but if you stop using parts, then parts will stop being delivered to you. The pull signals let the material delivery operator know what to deliver next, and in what quantity.

The number of pull signals in the system is based upon usage and delivery frequency, much, though not exactly, in the same way as the number of pull signals between the customer and supplier in a Lean enterprise system. The pull signals represent the information needed to deliver parts to the production floor. When an organization learns to effectively use pull signals to control and run its facility, it is able to make the transition to correctly developing suppliers into partners much easier, because it is already familiar with the pull signal as its information flow mechanism.

Route Development (Bus vs. Taxi)

In facilities that use this type of Lean internal material movement systems, the route is the final part of the system. The route is how the parts get from the purchased parts supermarket to the person that uses the parts. This system of internal material movement builds step by step until the actual delivery route runs. The PFEP provides the necessary information to size both the purchased parts supermarket and the number of pull signals in the information loop. The purchased parts supermarket serves as the central point of operation for the internal material movement system because it holds all of the purchased parts that will be delivered. The pull signals provide the information needed to deliver the correct parts to the correct area at the correct time.

Once your facility has a PFEP, a purchased parts supermarket, and pull signals, you'll know *what* material you need, *where* the material is stored, and *who* needs the material. Your next logical step, then, is to determine how to get the material from the supermarket to the production associate who needs the part in the most efficient way possible. We like to implement our internal material delivery systems like a bus route, not a taxi.

A taxi picks you up and takes you directly to where you want to go, drops you off, and charges you a fairly expensive fee. Then the taxi must drive around and look for another fare or be dispatched to another location. This action, we believe, resembles the movements of forklifts in many facilities; many forklifts deliver large amounts of inventory to one place, and then look for what is to be either delivered or picked up next.

A bus route, on the other hand, runs on a certain cadence. What gives you confidence to wait in the rain for the bus? If the cadence of the bus route is an hour, you can rest assured that the bus will be at the bus stop every hour.

Our goal is to design a delivery route that resembles a bus route, going through the production area and making the same stops every hour to determine if action needs to be taken. The pull signals tell the bus driver what needs to be delivered the next hour. After delivering product to the production associate, the bus driver retrieves any pull signals at the station and returns to the purchased parts supermarket to obtain the parts that correspond to those pull signals. Then the bus driver runs the route again, completing the same tasks as before. The consistency of this route provides stability to the facility by confirming to production that every hour (cadence), there will be a material delivery operator (bus driver) there to check on the status of production and make sure that production is supported in the way that is best for the facility.

A Few Final Thoughts Before We Get Started

An internal material movement system is important to external supplier development, as you will see described in this book. We felt it was necessary to outline the internal material movement system that we encourage most of the people that we work with to pursue, as there are references to parts of this system throughout this book.

It is important to have a solid internal material control system in place before attempting to implement Lean supplier development in your facility. The reason for this is because the internal material movement system will be the customer of the supplier development initiatives. Without a solid, stable customer, building a system of partnering with suppliers will be much more difficult.

We're not necessarily saying that this is the only way to effectively move material inside of your facilities, but we, and the people we work with, have had a great deal of success implementing and improving Lean internal material movement systems. Any system that you implement should be solid, stable, and efficient at both controlling and delivering material to the fingertips of the value-added operator.

The value-added operator actually adds value to the product. This is the person that makes something that you can sell to your customers. When any Lean enterprise system is developed, designed, and implemented, the value-added operator needs to be the focus. If the value-added operator isn't there to actually produce something of value that you can sell, everything else is useless. When designing a Lean enterprise system, always keep in mind that money is made where value is added, and that position should be optimized as much as possible.

The system of internal material movement that we have outlined in these few paragraphs was originally designed and developed to support value-added operators on the production floor. Although it has grown to be an inventory control system that allows facilities to force unneeded inventories out, it is still focused on the value-added operator. Therefore, developing a system or initiative to develop suppliers into partners based on enhancing and supporting the internal material movement system also supports the value-added processes and the value-added operators.

This book is written under the assumption that you have an internal material movement system based around optimizing the value-added operations, and that you are at a point in your internal material movement system where it could be enhanced by developing current suppliers into long-term partners!

Acknowledgments

Chris Harris: With great appreciation for the love, friendship, and support of my wife, Joie. I also thank my parents for a lifetime of opportunities and support. Also, with gratitude to all of our clients throughout the world that allow us to come into their facilities and learn with them. I also have a sincere appreciation for the faculty of the Falls School of Business at Anderson University in Anderson, Indiana.

Rick Harris: With gratitude to my wife, Ann, because without her belief in me, and her enduring love, none of this would have been possible. Thanks also to my sons, Christopher and Andrew, who make me proud to be a father every day, and to my parents, Albert and Fannie Mae, for instilling in me a good work ethic. Sincere appreciation must be accorded to Toyota, which introduced me to the Toyota Production System, and to all of the Harris Lean Systems clients throughout the world for allowing me to continue to learn.

Chuck Streeter: I thank my family for supporting me through the writing process, which was quite an experience. Lauren, Taylor, Carley, and CJ, I appreciate your understanding and the quiet time that you provided. Thank you, Joanne, for your encouragement and support, which allowed me to carve out yet another portion of my busy calendar to complete this work. I would like to especially thank my parents for teaching me dedication and determination. I also thank Rick and Chris for the opportunity to collaborate on this project.

We specifically thank Herb Bradshaw, first, for being such an excellent implementer of Lean principles; second, for allowing us to interview him for this book; and finally, for being a good friend to Harris Lean Systems. Thanks also to Chuck Streeter's daughter Lauren for her assistance in drawing some of the illustrations in this book.

Introduction: Why You Need This Book

The future holds a very different type of competition than what many of us are accustomed to. In the future, your facility won't be competing against your competitor's facility; your *supply chain* will be competing with your competitor's supply chain. In other words, the best supply chain wins!

This book will show you how to implement an essential aspect of a Lean supply chain: supplier development. If we are to develop a Lean supply chain and capitalize on a company's Lean improvements, we need to scrap our traditional way of looking at the supplier-customer relationship, and we need a new philosophy of supplier partnership to successfully compete in a global market. This book walks you through a step-by-step supply chain philosophy for companies looking to develop their supply chain into a Lean supply chain through supplier development. To accomplish this task, this book is broken into the following sections.

Section 1: Suppliers or Partners?

In this section, we'll discuss the overall philosophy of supplier development in a Lean supply chain. Is it better to have a supplier or a partner, and what's the distinction between the two?

We begin this section with an interview with a plant manager who has been successfully developing suppliers into partners for years. Since supplier development cannot happen in a silo, we'll also talk about the key players in supplier development in this section. When you develop suppliers, you impact different areas in a supply chain. It's important to identify those groups and begin to think about how developing suppliers is going to impact those individual groups as well as the supply chain. Finally, this section provides criteria on how to choose suppliers that would make good long-term partnerships.

Section 2: Internal Operations Essential to External Supplier Development

Your supply chain is only going to run as well as your facility runs, and it doesn't make a lot of sense to build an excellent supply chain around a broken process. Your facility's efficiency comes first; then, you can begin to build an efficient Lean supply chain.

In Section 2, we go into detail on how to identify the reasons that your facility's operations are vital to the performance of the overall supply chain. We'll also cover how to use Plan for Every Part (PFEP) to link your facility to the supply base, and we'll talk about the importance of a level schedule to an efficient Lean supply chain.

Section 3: The True Cost Model

Now that we understand the philosophy behind Lean supplier development and their importance to the supply chain, it is time to choose which suppliers should be developed into partners. Some people may say that global sourcing is the only thing that is going to save your company, while others say that global sourcing flies in the face of Lean supply chain methodology.

We say do the math and find out for sure. In Section 3, we'll present a true cost model and the methodology behind it, which you can use to develop your own true cost model. Then you can take all of the guesswork out of choosing which suppliers to develop and which ones are not worth the money or risk to develop. This section will look at various scenarios and situations that will hopefully help you as you develop a Lean supply base.

Section 4: Interactions between Lean Customers and Partners

Now that we have discussed the philosophy behind supplier development, its importance, and how to choose which suppliers to develop into partners, we can begin investigating how we will link to those partners. What is the pull loop size from the customer to the partner? What is a receiving board? What are receiving windows? What is your returnables versus disposable container philosophy?

These are some of the questions we'll answer in Section 4. This section builds on the previous three sections by showing you how to put mechanisms in place to ensure that once you choose a supplier to be developed into a partner, you will be able to effectively link to that partner, creating good, effective, and efficient information flow between you and your partner.

Section 5: Develop a Supplier into a Partner

This section takes it all to the next level. At this point, we know what a Lean partner should look like, why a Lean partner is important, how to choose a Lean partner, and how to link to a Lean partner. What we have left is how to develop the supplier into a partner.

This does not happen overnight. It takes time and effort, but it is something that can be done and pays off in a Lean supply chain. This section goes into detail on how to develop a supplier into a Lean partner.

Afterword

In this afterword, we wrap up all of the things that we have written about Lean supplier development in a Lean supply chain and provide general thoughts on how to continually improve a Lean supply chain.

Thank you for purchasing this book. Lean is a journey, not a destination, and we hope that you'll find *Lean Supplier Development* helpful on your personal Lean journey. We hope that by using the information in this book, you will look beyond the four walls of your facility and implement Lean systems in every facet of your business. We wish you the very best on your Lean journey. Never stop improving!

Best wishes,
Chris Harris, Rick Harris, and Chuck Streeter

The Authors

Dr. Chris Harris is a coauthor of the Shingo Prize-winning book *Making Materials Flow*, published by Jim Womack and the Lean Enterprise Institute. Chris has also coauthored two other books with Rick Harris, one on human resources' role in Lean manufacturing, entitled *Developing a Lean Workforce*, published by Productivity Press; and the other on the vital information flow in a production facility, entitled *Lean Connections*, also published by Productivity Press. Chris has also written many articles on Lean production systems.

Chris began his Lean manufacturing training as a team member on the assembly line at Toyota Motor Manufacturing Kentucky (TMMK). While at TMMK, the professionals taught Chris the proper use of TAKT time, standardized work, production status boards, and the utilization of Andon boards and the Andon system. Chris continued his Lean training at Toyota Tsusho America in Georgetown, Kentucky. Chris gained valuable hands-on experience in returnable containers, kanban card systems, supermarkets, milk runs, and Lean pricing. Chris realized the need to become knowledgeable in the implementation of Lean manufacturing in a unionized environment. Chris received this training as a front-line supervisor at Delphi Alternator Division in Anderson, Indiana, a UAW environment. While in this position, Chris gained a keen understanding of what is required to implement Lean manufacturing in a unionized environment. Dr. Harris decided to take another avenue and went into corporate purchasing at a tier 1 automotive company. In this position Chris learned the importance of purchasing's role in Lean production systems, and the effect of global purchasing on the enterprise value stream.

Chris has a doctorate in business administration from the Anderson University Falls School of Business in Anderson, Indiana. He is vice president of operations for Harris Lean Systems (www.harrisleansystems.com) and teaches workshops on various topics that assist companies on their Lean journey. Chris has spoken at the Lean Summit in Poland and has been a regular featured speaker for Jim Womack and the Lean Enterprise Institute.

 **Rick Harris** is the president of Harris Lean Systems and has been helping companies to become Lean for the past fifteen years. He has had great success helping large and small companies, union and nonunion, to implement their own Lean enterprise systems. HLS, Inc. has been instrumental in assisting companies worldwide with major cost reductions (a plant in New York, $42 million in four years; a plant in Indiana, $32 million in three years). He helps to educate executives, plant managers, and plant staff in the principles of Lean manufacturing. Rick helps with the actual implementation on the shop floor and the education of the workforce. He has pioneered the reverse flow process to achieve increases in efficiency of up to 25%. Rick has extensive experience in developing new manufacturing layouts that facilitate one-piece flow, operator flexibility, operator engagement, first time through quality, optimum uptime, and reduced capital investment. Rick has also coauthored the two Shingo Prize-winning books *Creating Continuous Flow* and *Making Materials Flow*, published by James Womack and the Lean Enterprise Institute. Rick has also coauthored two other books with his son, Dr. Chris Harris: *Developing a Lean Workforce* and *Lean Connections*, both published by Productivity Press. Rick has been one of the featured speakers at the Lean Enterprise Institute's monthly Lean conference. Rick has been a speaker at the University of Michigan Lean Manufacturing Conference, the Lean Enterprise Institute Summit, the European Lean Enterprise Institute Summit, the Maynard Forum, the PERA Conference, the Mississippi State Annual Lean Conference, the European AME Conference, the AME Conference in Chicago, the University of Kentucky Lean Leadership Forum, and the Lean Summit in Brazil.

Rick received his Lean training while serving as a manager in assembly at the Toyota plant in Georgetown, Kentucky. During his tenure at TMMK

Rick continued his Lean learning at the Toyota Tsutsumi Assembly Plant in Toyota City, Japan. He was a member of the start-up team at TMMK, where he gained extensive knowledge of the Toyota Production System. Prior to his Toyota experience, he spent fifteen years with General Motors. Rick began as a production operator and progressed through the ranks to become a first-line manager at General Motors. Rick is president of HLS, Inc.

Chuck Streeter is the owner of Streeter Lean Principles, LLC located in Indianapolis, Indiana. Chuck has worked with Rick Harris for over ten years, helping companies navigate through their Lean business system transformation journeys. Chuck gained much of his Lean knowledge working for companies in the automotive and electrical industries, with a majority of that being under the guidance of Rick Harris. In his various positions he was responsible for designing and implementing manufacturing processes and material delivery systems to transform from mass to Lean production processes in North America, Europe, and Asia. Chuck also led a development team in creating a total cost model to verify that Purchasing unequivocally understood the true cost of a part under sourcing review. As a Lean practitioner he has helped guide facilities to best improved, plant of the year, and corporate excellence accolades while instilling the principles of Lean in both their manufacturing and business processes.

Chuck gained his formal education with a bachelor of science in management from the U.S. Air Force Academy and a master of science in systems management from the Air Force Institute of Technology. Chuck is a level III certified acquisition program manager, as well as a retired commissioned officer in the U.S. Air Force Reserve.

SUPPLIERS OR PARTNERS?

Chapter 1

Does This Stuff Really Work?

Introduction

At the end of one of our three-day certificate events, someone asked: "Does this stuff really work?" The short answer is yes. But since you may not want to just take our word for it, we've decided to begin this book with an interview.

The Interview

We asked Herb Bradshaw, a successful Lean practitioner, if he would answer some questions for us to illustrate that the partnership philosophy can be successful and beneficial to a facility.

Herb Bradshaw is the plant manager of the Thomas & Betts Athens, Tennessee, facility. We've worked with the Athens Thomas & Betts facility since it began implementing the Lean philosophy in August 2001, and since then, the facility has won multiple honors, including being named one of *Industry Week*'s best plants in 2005. Through their supplier development and entire Lean Enterprise initiative, the facility has achieved the following impressive metrics:

- Consolidated over 327 suppliers into 104 partners
- 100% of key suppliers now certified
- 98% of all orders delivered on time to our request date

- 97% of all orders no longer require incoming inspection
- 85% of purchased material delivered on a just-in-time basis (daily)
- 90% of purchases on "supplier pull" tied to real-time customer demand pulls
- Reduced material handling costs by 45%, including 13 fork trucks
- Reduced average lead times from 18 days to 6.5 (goal is still 5 or less)
- Reduced average cycle times by 65%
- Improved raw/work-in-process (WIP) inventory turns, turns up from 11 to 110
- Improved finished goods turns, up from 4 to 12
- In-stock percent of finished goods improved from 82% to 98+%
- Eliminated 2,400 material handling totes, 260 bulk-packing hoppers, and opened up 75,000 square feet

We asked Herb a series of questions to find out how a partnership between the Thomas & Betts facility and their suppliers helped them to continually improve their production system.

Interview with Herb Bradshaw for Supplier Development Book: May 22, 2009

IN YOUR SITUATION, WHAT CAUSED THE NEED TO MOVE FROM A SUPPLIER MENTALITY TO A PARTNER MENTALITY?

When we began our Lean journey, I would not have considered us a highly respected customer to our supplier base. Like most other manufacturing organizations in the U.S., we were driven by sales forecasts. These forecasts, projections, and prognostications were never accurate by half. The direct result of manufacturing trying to react to unplanned, or revised, demand was the whipsawing of our supply base from expedite to de-expedite to expedite again. This process generated excess inventory at the supplier and within manufacturing. Ultimately, it also meant we had great excesses of finished goods filling warehouses, which most often was not what the customer was currently ordering or needed. Second, manufacturing's direct relationship with suppliers was censored and filtered through corporate level procurement groups. They were measured more by price than by service, delivery, or quality. We all know the result those conditions inflict on the stability of manufacturing processes.

Within a year of beginning our 2001 Lean journey, the Athens, Tennessee, operation was seeing very visible improvements. Material was beginning to flow, not stagnate; open floor space appeared as raw and in-process inventories fell, and service improved as finished inventories dropped. We owe our Lean education to Rick Harris and many of Harris Lean Systems' staff, who worked hand in hand with us since 2001 and continue to do so today.

Always looking to the next level, we obviously needed to convert our internal improvements into benefits our customers would appreciate. That path led us to focus on identifying the actual information flow of real-time customer demand (pull). Within that specific informational value stream were many elements of waiting, flow, and processing until demands were eventually satisfied. The key was to determine at what process point could the "voice of the customer" be heard, and then where a best-in-class response should be made. Manufacturing operations must become the strategic weapon in the transition to pull. The factory floor is where we made the best-in-class customer response.

Manufacturing getting its own house in order was the key to improved customer service and the key to stabilizing our processes, which in turn improved our supplier relationships.

In the second year of our Lean journey, our company began developing a true customer-driven pull system for order entry through distribution directly to manufacturing. Within two years, most manufacturing operations were flowing production in response to real-time customer demand. The next step, as the pull system tied to a legacy MRP2 for bill-of-material and routing files, was then to "pull" through the factories to first level suppliers for electronic ordering. Our supplier pull is a system that allows us to reach back in the supply chain with a fully integrated pull planning process from the customer through manufacturing to our partner suppliers.

We also had a change in management leadership in corporate procurement that reestablished supplier relationships at the plant level and established a partnership between corporate and plant procurement teams. Decisions were now being made on total cost, not just price.

HOW WOULD YOU DEFINE A SUPPLIER?

Any organization that provides a component, product, or service needed to support the successful and profitable manufacture of your company's products. Generic definitions would include adjectives like *manufacturer* or *producer*; in-service support like subcontractor, provider, or source; and material brokers materials like retailer, wholesaler, merchant, and vendor. Much as these descriptions sound impersonal, so then is the relationship.

HOW WOULD YOU DEFINE A PARTNER?

The obvious difference here is that the relationship with a business partner is basically *not* impersonal. A partner becomes a colleague, collaborator, and teammate. We join forces and work together to the benefit of both. A partner brings to the table knowledge and expertise in his or her processes and products. Since most manufacturers are not vertically integrated from raw material to finished products, business partners must be utilized to provide those resources. Some basic elements must include the following:

Narrow the field: Fewer suppliers allow for more effective communication, and information flow and fewer suppliers, each with more volume, will generate lower total costs.
Mutually beneficial relationships will provide stronger partnerships.
Calculate total cost: Service, quality, sharing improvement savings, collaborating on product development, and all aspects of the partnership—not just price!

HOW MANY SUPPLIERS DID YOU TURN IN TO PARTNERS, AND WHAT IS THE SIZE OF YOUR CURRENT SUPPLY BASE COMPARED TO BEFORE THE CHANGE?

Stability in our own processes generated creditability in the pull process with suppliers. Accurate PFEP (Plan for Every Part) was essential. About year 3 of our Lean journey, we began serious talks with key commodity providers about where we were going as a company and how the future state vision looked. They were skeptical. Fortunately, we found suppliers in each component family curious enough to listen to our story of improvement and with the capability to become a partner.

We began with about 325 suppliers of raw material and components. By the end of 2004, we were down to 104 suppliers. We had firmly established six supply partners that provided over 50% of our raw material purchase dollars.

WHAT ARE THE BENEFITS THAT YOU HAVE SEEN IN MOVING FROM THE CLASSIC SUPPLIER MENTALITY TO A PARTNERSHIP STRATEGY?

Through our Lean journey, we have believed that we are both a better supplier to our customers and a better customer to our suppliers by truly focusing on what the customer wanted—expected—"the golden rule"—and building strong, mutually beneficial relationships with our suppliers. Most of your customers will pay for and accept:

- Simple, focused, and responsive order processing
- Industry-best lead times
- Highly flexible production processes
- Consistent shipments and coordinated deliveries
- Perfect quality
- Production flow accelerating cash flow
- Mutually profitable partnerships

Every one of these points applies to our relationship with our customers as well as our supply partners.

Our partner suppliers have participated in kaizen events and training classes on Lean fundamentals. They have adopted many Lean principles into their organizations.

HAVE YOU EVER SOURCED A COMPONENT AT A HIGHER PIECE PRICE COST BECAUSE IT WAS CHEAPER AS A WHOLE FOR THE VALUE STREAM (PLEASE EXPLAIN)?

Yes, we have sourced product at a higher piece price several times. Although it was not in place until 2007, we now have a tool that helps us relate the value of many delivery aspects to piece price across multiple potential sources. Our TAC (total acquisition cost) modeler takes into account the value of lead time, payment terms, piece price, freight cost, transit time, in-transit inventory value, customs fees, and import duties and taxes. Subjective elements are considered in qualification of the supplier's quality to eliminate the cost of receiving inspection and service performance versus promise dates to reduce safety stocks.

IN YOUR FACILITY, WHAT ORGANIZATIONS WERE VITAL TO CHANGING TO A PARTNERSHIP MENTALITY?

As we began to formulate a definition for a partner rather than a supplier, it was obvious that every aspect of our business would be positively affected through that transformation. When you think about a partner supplier, they should make every step of procurement, from ordering through receipt and payment, easier. Purchasing, receiving, quality, inventory control, planning, scheduling, production, and accounts payable functions are affected by each transaction. They are willing to communicate electronically, respond consistently and timely, and ship product straight to the production floor without need for inspection. They also know the implications for a failure in any aspect of the relationship and are quick to respond, take responsibility, and set assurances to prevent reoccurrence.

We have worked with component supply partners to utilize a shipping carton to our specifications that can in turn be reused to package our finished product. We have jointly worked to eliminate excess packaging material, saving the suppliers money and reducing tons of trash we paid to have landfilled. A supplier provided expertise to redesign a component that reduced material content and reduced the piece price. We helped a supply partner get over the anxiety of removing some just-in-case inventory through kanban training, and we shared in the savings of eliminating a leased building.

WHO WERE THE KEY PLAYERS?

In our organization every department became involved, participated, and was impacted by the favorable relationships with supply partners.

WITH YOUR CURRENT PARTNERSHIP STRATEGY, HOW DOES THE FUTURE LOOK FOR YOU AND YOUR PARTNERS?

Sorry, no crystal balls around here. I think that the next few years are going to be a true test of our ability to sustain these relationships. The advantage is that we have been consistent and truthful in our relationships and that will carry a lot of weight down the road.

Two of the original supply partners we developed for our facility have now been successful in expanding their sales to multiple facilities within our company, replacing other suppliers.

HOW HAVE YOUR PARTNERS RECEIVED THE NEW STRATEGY?

All except one of the original suppliers that became partners, at least by definition, are still working closely with us. The one exception was a commodity supplier purchased by a foreign company that then eliminated a key finishing process of our product. The fact that they all benefited from substantially more business in volume and sales certainly helped strengthen the relationship.

After the initial supply partners were established, we began a more formal program of supplier development. We have averaged one additional program each quarter since 2006. We base the supplier's selection on several criteria and consider the total value of purchase dollars, whether they're a sole source, and whether the item, or process, is proprietary, etc.

CAN YOU TELL A DIFFERENCE IN THE WAY THAT THE PARTNERS INTERACT WITH YOUR ORGANIZATION?

I guess that from the answers above the obvious response is yes. Of the other ten to twelve companies we have worked with on supplier development in the last two years, a couple have not embraced the concepts. They have remained good suppliers, but they have not been willing to change processes or philosophies to adopt Lean philosophies. They may not always be suppliers to us. Our corporate level procurement group has held an annual meeting of thirty to forty high-value suppliers to discuss our overall guiding principles and both short- and long-term goals and objectives. By far our facilities' partner suppliers are the best represented. They have actually presented case studies on their own development journey working with us.

Thanks to Herb for taking the time to answer these questions and to illustrate for you, readers, that these practices really do work. Throughout this book, we'll cover many of the practices and strategies that Herb has mentioned.

So, does this stuff really work? Yes. It's worked for Herb and for our other clients, and it can work for you. When implemented at the proper time and implemented well, supplier development is an excellent way to catapult your Lean improvement initiatives to a whole other level.

When you begin to think in terms of supply chains and not just in terms of your facility, you are beginning to think globally. That mentality will serve you well, as the world gets smaller and smaller.

The remainder of this book is written in a way to help you get started and continue to develop your suppliers into long-term partnerships. The next chapter specifically discusses a Lean supplier development philosophy.

Chapter 2

The Supplier Development Philosophy

Introduction

In a global and rapidly changing economy, the classic lowest piece price cost purchasing philosophy detracts from your competitive edge. Instead, the purchasing process in a Lean enterprise needs to be based on supplier development and implemented with the entire corporation and the entire corporation's supply chain in mind. Good supplier partnerships often lead to lower total cost and higher quality, making supplier development a win-win for both the supplier and the customer.

If you have spent time working with value streams in your facility, you will likely find that the principles of improving the supply chain are the same. For example, let's look inside a typical manufacturing facility that has a stamping department, paint department, and final assembly department. Oftentimes, facilities will take a simplistic approach to improving and focusing on improving the stamping department, the paint department, and the final assembly department, all individually. That makes sense in the old mass manufacturing mentality. Lean enterprise facilities, however, need to examine the entire value stream that encompasses the stamping department, paint department, and final assembly department.

A facility that understands how all of the different departments in a facility fit together to efficiently serve the customer will make decisions based upon that value stream, and not on any one individual department. Similarly, as you develop suppliers for your Lean enterprise, your goal will be to improve the entire supply chain.

Two Different Philosophies

We have worked in traditional mass manufacturing environments as well as in environments that are far along on their Lean journey. The two environments have drastically different philosophies. In the classic mass manufacturing environment, you run with high inventories, large lot sizes, and little flexibility. In Leaner environments, there is a constant push to reduce inventories, decrease lot sizes, and increase flexibility. As you'd expect, their supplier development philosophies are also drastically different.

In a mass manufacturing environment piece price usually drives the selection of the supplier, often leading to a supply base that is spread throughout many suppliers all over the world. This philosophy can cause great difficulty in the production process. Take, for example, the following scenario.

You are the corporate purchasing agent in charge of purchasing plastic components for the entire corporation. Your key performance measurement in your position is piece price cost. Over the years, we've learned that behavior is almost always driven by measurements; if your job success is measured on getting the lowest piece price cost, you will look for the lowest piece price cost under most circumstances. Your bonus, future promotions, and yearly raise are all tied to how well you obtain the lowest piece price cost for the plastic components.

Let's say that you buy twenty separate plastic components for your facility. Each time that you send a quotation out to your potential plastic suppliers, a new supplier comes back with a lower piece price cost. Therefore, you have twenty different suppliers that supply you plastic components. Let's illustrate this point (see Figure 2.1).

Proponents of this type of global purchasing, or lowest piece price philosophy, either believe that it is best to be diversified in your supply base, or do not care about the supply base at all and are only concerned with piece price cost. They think that if they are well diversified, it will be much more difficult for one of their suppliers to hurt them if they do not ship the product, ship a bad quality product, or are shut down by a natural (or manmade) disaster. However, this may not be the case.

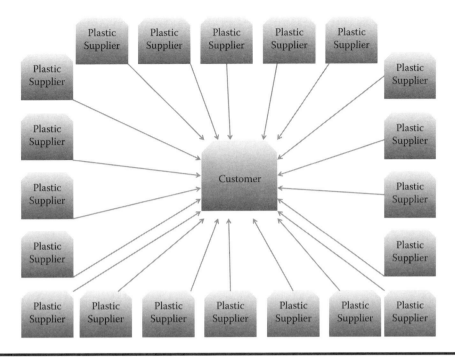

Figure 2.1   Classic low-cost supply base.

Looking at the previous philosophy and understanding the actual functionality of it can certainly cause some rather large problems. For example, how many of the twenty plastic component suppliers need to stop shipping you product to shut down your production? The answer is only one. So, it is safe to say that all twenty of the suppliers hold the success of your facility in their hands to some degree. In other words, they control you in a sense, because if they decide not to ship you product, they can shut you down.

You may be thinking at this point that since they're your suppliers, they will always ship you a good product. Unfortunately, that's not necessarily the case. Let's say that the first supplier that you sourced a plastic component with sends in a component that has a problem. You call that supplier up and tell them that they need to come in to your facility to remedy the quality problem right away.

What incentive does that supplier have to come to your facility and fix the quality problem? They have tried to win the business on nineteen other, separate plastic components since they won their first plastic component. They realize that there is very little chance that they will ever get the business on another plastic component from your company. They are also just breaking even on the original part that won the quotation. They were just trying to get in the door with the first part, so they quoted the component as low as they possibly could in the hopes that future business would come their way, but it never did.

The supplier has very little incentive to help you out with the quality problem that they created. Consider that the supplier is likely thousands of miles away from you, and you have a real problem. Now you will likely have to begin sorting the product as it comes in the door (if you weren't already), and order more quantity of the component to cover the pieces that have quality problems.

In this situation, the supplier can really hurt you as a production facility, even if they only supply one component to your facility. They have very little incentive to take good care of you, so they continue to produce the product to fill their production, but are not willing to go the extra mile to service their customer. In reality, this is a one-way relationship. You need them, but they can do without you.

Our Lean purchasing philosophy plays out much differently.

Let's say that you are the same purchasing agent in charge of buying all of the plastic components for your corporation. But this time, instead of continually going out to chase the lowest piece price, you are charged with finding one plastic components supplier with whom to develop a long-term relationship.

A key ingredient to successful supplier development is an understanding that *your organization is going to only be as healthy as your supply base!* Just imagine if your supply base went out of business tomorrow. What if even just one of your suppliers went out of business tomorrow? Pure chaos. Good organizations using Lean enterprise systems understand the importance of the supply base and develop the supply side of their enterprise accordingly.

Let's assume that you take this approach of developing suppliers, rather than using the classic purchasing mentality. In this environment, you are not evaluated on piece price alone, but on how successful you are at developing suppliers into effective Lean partners. Take a look at the impact of this approach on the Lean enterprise (see Figure 2.2).

In this situation, only one plastics supplier supplies all of the plastic components for your corporation. Because you're only using one supplier, and therefore placing larger orders, your organization is likely a big portion of the plastic supplier's customer base. Therefore, if you have a quality problem with a component, it is much more likely that the supplier will get to your facility very quickly. The relationship relies on the success of both parties: your supplier needs to do well if you are to succeed, and you need to do well if your supplier is to succeed.

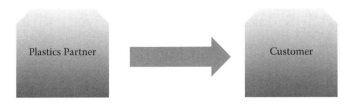

Figure 2.2 Supplier-partner link.

In this relationship, both the customer and the supplier need to make decisions that are best for the supply chain as a whole, versus what is best for the individual facilities. In the future, competition will not be facility versus facility or company versus company, but will be a facility or company's supply chain versus its competitor's supply chain; as a result, you'll need a different methodology for making supplier and purchasing decisions.

In our scenario where we have only one plastic parts supplier:

1. Does the transportation become less costly and cumbersome if you only have to coordinate transportation to (returning containers) and from one supplier?
2. Does the possibility of more frequent deliveries, which allows a facility to carry less inventory, become a more plausible situation?
3. Does a change to standard size returnable containers that enable better internal material movement become much more feasible?
4. Does this relationship make it easier to go to the supplier (partner) and request different standard packs that coincide with your finished goods quantity?

The answer to all of these questions is yes, and then some. There are additional benefits that come with this philosophy, and throughout the remainder of the book, we'll tell you what they are and why this philosophy of supplier (partner) development is the right direction for companies implementing Lean enterprise initiatives. Is your organization ready to move in this direction? Come along with us, and we'll show you how.

Conclusion

The classic mentality of letting the lowest piece price cost be the single most important factor in sourcing decisions is, has been, and will continue to be a detriment to good Lean facilities throughout the United States and the world. It's time for a different thought process and a different take on competition.

In the future, competition in a global market is not going to be my facility versus your facility; it's not going to be my labor cost versus your labor cost; and it's probably not going to be my raw material cost versus your raw material cost in the future. Future competition, almost certainly, will be my complete supply chain versus your complete supply chain.

No longer can you simply source product with suppliers. It's time for a paradigm shift: What decision is best for the supply chain in the long term? The best supply chain wins!

Chapter 3

Key Players in Supplier Development

Introduction

To tackle supplier development, you need to assemble the right team of people with the right type of knowledge. In this chapter, we'll outline some of the key organizations that need to be involved in the supplier development initiative.

First, we'll talk about the importance of good communication between key players. Then, we'll discuss each of the key organizations in supplier development, and illustrate some common problems associated with a lack of communication between the organizations—and how you can avoid them.

The Importance of Communication among Key Players

There are a few organizations that are key to a successful supplier development initiative. These organizations need to work closely together so that the decisions that are made are right for the entire facility or company and not just the organization making the decision. The following example illustrates this point.

When material is moved from one facility to another, we call this plant-to-plant material movement. Plant-to-plant material movement is illustrated by a triangle of involvement, which represents the key players (Figure 3.1).

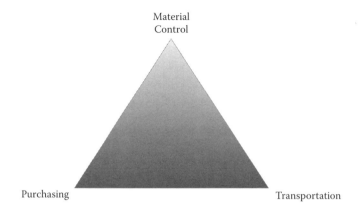

Material
Control

Purchasing   Transportation

Figure 3.1   Plant-to-plant triangle of involvement.

The first key player is the purchasing organization. In many companies, purchasing is measured solely by the piece price cost of the component they are sourcing. In other words, the lower the piece price cost that the purchasing agents get, the better their evaluations, or the better they are perceived to be at their job. Keeping that in mind, purchasing agents are asked to source their most recent widget and are presented with the following three quotations:

Quotation 1: Supplier A	15 cents	Distance away: 5 miles
Quotation 2: Supplier B	14 cents	Distance away: 500 miles
Quotation 3: Supplier C	13 cents	Distance away: 5,000 miles

Again, behavior is driven by measurements. If the purchasing agent wants to excel in his job, he'll choose supplier C, because that is the lowest piece price quoted for the widget. In this case, the measurement is the lowest piece price cost; therefore, the purchasing agent chooses supplier C even though it's 5,000 miles away. By the current measurements, the purchasing agent has done an outstanding job.

The next organization to become involved is transportation. Once the part is sourced, the transportation agent needs to determine how the component will get from the supplier to the customer. Transportation is also measured on cost, and has had no input into the sourcing of the component; they are just charged with getting the component from the supplier to the facility as inexpensively as possible. The transportation agent is presented with the following quotations for the transportation of the widget from supplier C to the facility:

One shipment per day: $500	($10,000 per month)
One shipment per week: $2,000	($8,000 per month)
One shipment every six months: $24,000	($4,000 per month)

In our example, the transportation agent chooses to get a shipment every six months because it's the cheapest on a per-month basis. Once again, the measurements in the organization have driven the behavior of the employees, as is almost always the case. Now that the widget is sourced, and the transportation of the widget has been arranged, the responsibility moves to the third organization in the triangle of involvement—material control.

Material control is, quite simply, in charge of controlling the material in the facility. When facility management wants inventory levels lowered, they go to the material control organization and ask them to reduce the inventory levels. Suppose for a moment that this happens in our scenario: management approaches the material control department and tells them to lower inventory levels on a widget that they receive every six months, from about 5,000 miles away. It is very difficult to reduce inventory levels in this scenario, since each shipment brings in six months of inventory; further, to protect yourself from unforeseen problems, you are likely going to carry a large safety stock.

In short, the silo management approach here leads to a very dangerous situation for an organization. In this scenario, it would be possible for purchasing to "save" the company a million dollars, and transportation to "save" the company a million dollars. But this approach actually *costs* the company money based on inventory cost, storage costs, possible quality problems, obsolete parts, etc., whereas if we could get the purchasing agent, transportation agent, and material control agent in a room together where they could talk, and change their measurement objectives from the lowest cost to purchasing and transportation, to the lowest cost for the entire organization, the decision would likely be very different.

By now, you can see how important measurement tools and communication are within a company or facility. In the realm of supplier development, there are certain organizations and departments that must be involved and communicate to form a successful initiative to develop partnerships in a Lean supply chain.

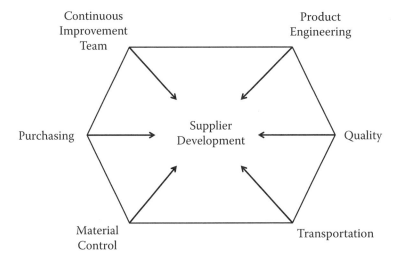

Figure 3.2 Key players to supplier development.

Key Players in Supplier Development

Nobody has said that developing suppliers into partners is easy, but it will go more smoothly if you have the right organizations involved in the process from the outset. The following list may not be all-inclusive, but it can get you started developing suppliers into partners (Figure 3.2).

Continuous Improvement Team

If you haven't already formed a continuous improvement team within your organization, now's the time. Your continuous improvement team is a group of individuals that are very important in the implementation of your Lean initiatives in your facility. This group needs to understand how your system was developed, implemented, and currently works. Remember, you are developing suppliers into partners to support your Lean enterprise system, so this group of individuals needs to have extensive knowledge of how your system was put together and how it works.

The optimal continuous improvement team will have a representative from manufacturing, management, internal material movement, scheduling, the hourly workforce, and industrial engineering. Collectively, this team possesses valuable knowledge: knowledge that you need as you choose suppliers and develop them into long-term partners.

Purchasing

Purchasing needs to be involved in this process for two reasons. The first, and most obvious, reason is that they are the people who actually purchase the product. Second, they have an invaluable knowledge of how suppliers are currently dealt with within the organization. When you explain your new philosophy of partner development to your purchasers, and give them the support that they need to implement it, they will become an integral part of the supplier development process.

We can't emphasize enough how important purchasing is to this process. They must be on board, and they need to understand our approach to developing suppliers into partners. One item that we need to address early in the process is the measurement targets currently placed on the purchasing department.

As long as purchasing is measured by piece price cost alone, we will always have problems making decisions that are right for the entire organization. We have worked in environments where this was the case, and in environments where this was not the case, and the differences are staggering. Take, for example, the role of a value stream manager,* in which a manager does not manage individual departments within the stream of value, but manages the stream of value as a whole (Figure 3.3).

In this case, the value stream manager will make decisions that are best for the entire value stream, and not just an individual department. What if you have a purchasing agent in charge of the entire value stream, measured based on the efficiency and effectiveness of that value stream? Do you think the sourcing decisions would be different? Do you think that the purchasing agent would actively seek input from those in production on how to make the value stream more efficient and effective?

This is a different way to think about how components are purchased. However you choose to go about involving your purchasing department, it is important to get them involved early and often, and make sure that you take advantage of their knowledge as you move toward your supplier development goals.

But what about corporate purchasing versus localized purchasing? A corporate purchasing department is separated from the facility and purchases components for all of the facilities in the company. For example, you may have an off-site corporate buyer who purchases all of the plastic components

---

* Rother, R., and J. Shook, **Learning to See: Value Stream Mapping to Create Value and Eliminate Muda** (Brookline, MA: Lean Enterprise Institute, 1998).

Figure 3.3   A value stream manager's responsibility.

for the entire company, rather than a person dedicated solely to your facility's components.

The argument for corporate purchasing rallies around the concept of synergies, meaning that they can bring the entire demand of a component or types of components or commodities (e.g., plastic components) for the entire company together to receive discounts. On paper, this purchase price variance, or piece price cost, may look like a very good idea. However, as we'll illustrate later, in Section 3, just because a component has a low piece price cost does not necessarily mean that it is the best decision for the facility as a whole.

Localized purchasing, conversely, places a purchasing agent within your facility, or at least dedicated to your facility. In this instance, important variables, such as component packaging and delivery frequency, can be considered when purchasing components. Partnerships may also be easier to form between facilities and supplier in a localized purchasing situation.

Each type of purchasing can have its advantages and disadvantages, and these are largely situational. If you have a large organization, then obviously you want to take advantage of volume discounts, because that will likely be best for your company. Our advice is to find a way to negotiate with the supplier volume discounts for the entire company, but allow each individual facility to choose their method of receiving the material from the standpoint of packaging, frequency of delivery, etc. This can provide your organization the best of both worlds, so to speak, allowing for volume discounts as well as the flexibility for individual facilities to dictate how they want to receive the material.

Material Control

Your material control department is very important to the process of supplier development as well, because these employees know how to move the material inside of the facility. If yours is like many of the facilities that we help implement Lean enterprise systems, you do a lot of repacking once the components reach your facility. The reason that this happens, in the current state, is because the packaging and quantities that arrive from current suppliers are not suitable for the Lean internal material system. In the future, we hope that there will be no repacking because we can work with partners to develop the right packaging and quantities that optimize the Lean internal movement system. The group that knows which packaging and quantities that they would like to have in each box to optimize the Lean internal material movement system is the material control organization: the group in charge of operating the internal movement of material.

In any organization, money is made as the value flows from the beginning of the process to the customer. Material control inside of a facility is vital to making the material, or value, flow throughout the facility. Therefore, it is very important to recognize that we are developing suppliers not only to support production efforts, but more specifically, to support the material flow system in the facility.

It is equally important that you take advantage of the knowledge base of the material control organization within your facility. Once again, this organization has an area of expertise necessary to effectively develop suppliers. We need to make sure that we capitalize on their knowledge base; remember, material control is an organization that we are going to support with the supplier development initiatives and develop suppliers into partners accordingly. The customer of the supplier development program is the internal material movement system in your facility. Your supplier development program will support the material control department's efforts to continually improve.

Product Engineering

Product engineering is the term that we use for the group that designs future products for your organization. You may use another term for this organization (for example, *research and development*), but you most certainly have a group of people in charge of designing future products and identifying the purchased components needed for that product. Why include this group in supplier development? Because they need to let the rest of the key players in this process know precisely what they need from a supplier or suppliers. Further, your product engineers need to know what capabilities the supply base has. The supply base may have core capabilities that your product engineering or research and development team is looking for, or a similar capability that can be used at lower cost—all of which can influence product design.

Too many times, product engineers are not involved in the Lean process, both from the beginning of Lean implementation and moving forward. You'll find that your employees get really frustrated when they receive a product from product engineering that is difficult to assemble, but your product engineering group can hardly be faulted when they're not asked or given the knowledge necessary to design a product to be produced in a Lean enterprise. What are your company's Lean product design criteria?

For the long-term success of your Lean enterprise, you need to get the organization that designs your future products involved in all phases of Lean implementation. Otherwise, five years from now your situation won't have changed, and you'll find yourself trying to figure out how to produce a product designed with little thought put into how to actually produce the product.

Quality

One of the more frustrating things that we hear when we talk with people about supplier development is the percentage of components that they have to inspect when they are received from their suppliers. When a facility receives components from a supplier, the products should be ready to use, with no need for inspection.

When you begin to create partnerships within your supply chain, you discover fairly quickly which suppliers are unable to provide high-quality parts, on time, and obviously, you won't want to pursue partnerships with these particular suppliers. Instead, you'll pursue partnerships with organizations that currently deliver very high quality components, or which have quality control systems in place to ensure high quality.

For these reasons, you need to involve the quality organization in the supplier development process. The quality organization should be able to recommend suppliers that are good choices to develop into partners. One of the biggest disruptions to the flow of value is poor quality, and with the goal of effective and efficient flow of value, quality from suppliers is a must. We have all heard the line "garbage in, garbage out," and it rings true in processes as well. If we have bad components coming into the process, it will be very difficult to create good products at the end of the process.

Transportation

Once your supply chain partnerships are formed, transportation becomes very important, since they're the organization in charge of getting the product from the supplier to the facility in an efficient manner. The key word here is *efficient*. When we say *efficient*, we mean efficient within the context of a Lean supply chain. This may mean more frequent deliveries. With more frequent deliveries come lower inventories and higher efficiencies, but more frequent deliveries can also lead to higher transportation costs.

Obviously, you'll want to keep all of your costs, including transportation, as low as possible. But even if transportation costs go up, your total costs may well go down. When you're developing suppliers into partners, you need to discuss and reach consensus on all possible scenarios. And because transportation is an important part of a supply chain, they too should be involved in the supplier development process within a Lean supply chain. Bringing them in will ensure that when components are moved from the supplier to the facility, the process is smooth and efficient.

The Role of the Key Players (The Advisory Team)

Your key players will form an *ad hoc* advisory team. In Section 5, we'll talk about how to actually develop suppliers into partners, and your advisory team will then provide you with the information you need to choose the correct suppliers to develop, and to give input into improving how the supplier interacts with the facility.

Collectively, the key players outlined in this chapter hold a great deal of knowledge. If you can get them all in one room, discussing one subject, you can accomplish great things in the area of supply chain improvement and supplier development. So bring them together once a week at the outset of implementation, and once a month later in the process. However you get this group together, realize that the sharing of this knowledge is vital to the long-term success of your supply chain.

Conclusion

By now, you can see how critical communication among key players is to implementation of your supplier development process—and which players need to be involved. It really doesn't matter how intelligent and good your people are in these organizations; if you are not developing systems to obtain and share their collective knowledge in the context of Lean supplier development, you are not getting the value out of the organizations that you could be getting. The remainder of this book assumes that you have a good team assembled to accomplish the task of development of suppliers into partners, so it is probably a good idea to begin thinking about your team as you read this book.

These people don't make up our system, but the information that these individuals hold is *vital* to developing our system of supplier development. Remember, a good Lean organization gets brilliant results from brilliant processes run by average people, while other companies try to get brilliant results from brilliant people with broken processes. Our goal is to develop a brilliant supplier development process!

Chapter 4

How to Choose a Supplier for a Long-Term Partnership

Introduction

Now that you're familiar with the philosophy of Lean supplier development and the key players involved, we'll talk about some of the attributes that need to be considered when choosing a supplier to form a long-term partnership.

This chapter identifies ten attributes to consider when choosing a supplier with whom to form a long-term partnership. Although the list in this chapter may not be all-encompassing, it will provide you with a foundation and strategies for choosing suppliers to develop into long-term partners, which you can then use to develop your own attributes.

Who Chooses the Suppliers to Develop?

This is where your key players, or advisory team, come in. As we discuss the attributes to consider when choosing a supplier to develop, you'll see that there is a lot of information needed, and your key players will be in place to provide input and vital information about the suppliers *and* the needs of your organization. To make the proper decisions, you need the right information about potential supplier-partners.

Attribute 1: Attitude

Does the supplier want to partner with your organization? This is a good question to ask—and answer—in the beginning of the process. If the supplier's attitude seems anti-long-term partnership, then you should probably look for another supplier to develop.

A positive attitude from a supplier can go a long way toward the success of a long-term partnership. If a supplier wants to form a long-term partnership, then it will likely be willing to work on addressing the remaining nine attributes discussed in this chapter.

So, how do you ascertain a supplier's attitude? It's very straightforward: talk to them. Find out what they think. If you believe that they are sincerely committed to forming a long-term partnership, then you've likely satisfied the most important attribute for choosing a supplier for a long-term partnership.

Attribute 2: Quality Level

The next attribute that you need to consider when choosing a supplier with whom to form a long-term partnership is *quality*. If the quality of your incoming material is substandard, your operations will be less efficient and your end product is likely to be inferior. Incoming inspection at your facility needs to become a thing of the past due to excellent quality of incoming material.

How is the supplier's quality? Does the supplier have a long history of good quality or a long history of poor quality? Quality is vital to good flow in your manufacturing facility, and if a supplier cannot provide good quality, it is very difficult for that supplier to become a good candidate for a long-term partnership.

Attribute 3: Capacity

Does the supplier have the capacity to support your facility? Sometimes a supplier may look like a good prospect for a long-term partnership, but just doesn't possess the production capacity that you need now—and in the future.

Although you certainly want to ensure that any supplier-partner you choose has the capacity to support you now, it is also critical to think about the future. The supplier may have the capacity to support you now, but what about in five years? Will it be able to support your facility, or does it at least have a growth strategy that will get it in a position where it can support you in the future? These are important questions because you certainly do not want to have to begin looking for another supplier to partner with in the future because of a lack of capacity.

Attribute 4: Vital Expertise

Does your potential partner have a vital expertise or core competency that you require? There are certainly products and tasks that many facilities need that they do not—or cannot—perform themselves. We have worked with many different companies that are really good at producing their product, but producing that product requires a vital process or component that they cannot produce or create themselves.

If your facility requires a vital component or outside process, then by definition you need it to continue to produce that product. This situation does limit your options somewhat. You have to partner with this supplier, live with the current supplier relationship as is, find a new supplier, or cease to use the process or component.

Since your options are limited, the other attributes may become less of an issue. If you have to have the component or process, then you have to find the best method to deal with the supplier. Therefore, proceed with caution, understanding that this may not be the most optimal situation for creating a partnership. Again, if the supplier has a core competency that you can't find elsewhere, you'll need to pursue that partnership to the best of your organization's ability, using and adapting the information in the following chapters however possible.

Attribute 5: On-Time Delivery

When a product is consistently not delivered on time, it drives the inventory levels at your facility higher. This happens because your facility has to plan for delivery not being on time. For example, if the shipment is a day late 50% of the time, your facility must carry extra inventory to cover the anticipated late deliveries, holding more inventory than would be necessary if the material were delivered on time. On-time delivery can play an important role in the success of a Lean enterprise system, so it is important to consider when choosing a supplier to form a long-term partnership.

Does your supplier have an on-time delivery problem? If so, then it is not a good choice for a long-term relationship. On-time shipping has implications for your entire supply chain, and as such, it is very important for your facility that shipments are shipped and received when they are supposed to be shipped and received.

Attribute 6: Payment Terms (Pay on Pull)

Does the supplier have favorable payment terms? Does your supplier have a vendor-managed mentality? Will they allow your facility to pay on pull (in other words, charge you only when you pull the product from the supplier)?

If your facility can pull on a consistent basis, then the supplier can plan accordingly and will likely allow you to pay on pull. However, if your facility is not stable enough to pull in a level, balanced, and consistent manner, then your supplier would have to guess when you were going to actually pull. That would likely place a lot of pressure on the supplier's production system, leading to higher cost and inefficiencies. In short, the payment terms need to be appropriate for both parties. Without a solid supply base, your facility cannot function, so you need to come to a mutually beneficial situation with your supplier. Can you get there with the supplier with whom you are thinking about forming a long-term partnership?

Attribute 7: Credit Standing

Does your potential partner have a good credit rating? Is the supplier financially healthy? Is the supplier viable in the long term?

When forming a long-term partnership, you need to consider whether the supplier is going to be around for a long time, or whether they're barely hanging on right now. If a supplier is barely hanging on, they are likely to tell you everything that you want to hear to get your business. Finding out the company's credit rating is a form of investigation that gives you objective information about the company and its leadership. What does the credit rating tell you about the supplier? Will the supplier allow you to look at its financials? What other things can you do to determine how healthy the supplier is now? What can you do to determine the supplier's long-term prospects? This attribute is important because you do not want to put a lot of work into developing a supplier that is going to go out of business in the next five years.

Attribute 8: Volume Commodity

Is your facility part of a corporation with many facilities? If so, does the corporation buy a lot of a certain commodity? In this instance, it would make sense for the corporation to capitalize on volume pricing, which leads us to our next question: Can the corporation buy the commodity from the same supplier?

If the answer is yes, you need to consider whether that supplier will make a good partner. Volume price breaks aren't enough; the supplier also needs to be willing to work with each individual facility to deliver the commodity in a manner that is best for the facility.

Many times we have seen volume contracts negotiated with minimum buy quantities and the method of delivery (frequency, size, etc.) determined by the supplier. In this situation, the supplier will make decisions that are best for the supplier alone, because the contract has already been negotiated with no thought to how the facilities need to receive the commodity to operate most efficiently. This often leads to large lot sizes and infrequent deliveries—clearly not something we want to see in a Lean enterprise.

Why can't you have both? If your supplier is willing to both give you the corporate volume discounts and work with each individual facility to provide the best manner of delivery for its Lean enterprise system, then a partnership with the supplier may well be worth pursing.

Attribute 9: Flexibility to Package

The packaging of incoming components is critical to the internal material movement in a facility. How flexible is the supplier willing to be with regards to packaging?

Any supplier you're considering developing into a partner needs to be willing to give you the component that you are purchasing in the manner in which you would like to receive the component. However, it is not the supplier's responsibility to determine the best way for your facility to receive the product; it is your responsibility to determine the right quantity and container size for the component, and it is also important that this does not change all of the time. Constant changes in packaging specifications can put a lot of stress on the supplier's production system and can erode their confidence and trust in your facility, which isn't a good situation for anyone. If you are tweaking your system or continually improving your system, try different box sizes and quantities internally to be sure that they are correct before requiring your suppliers to change.

Nonetheless, it is important to choose a supplier that is open to changing on occasion if it is in the best interest of the supply chain as a whole.

Attribute 10: True Cost Model Standing

True cost models provide you with the true cost of sourcing a product. Though cost is not the sole determinant of sourcing decisions in a Lean enterprise environment, it will likely always be a very important one.

In Section 3, we'll talk about how to develop a true cost model. Once you've developed your model, it can show you how the costs add up with one supplier versus another supplier, and to determine the true cost of a sourcing decision. If used consistently, you will likely see patterns of cost that may lead you to a supplier that has potential for a long-term partnership.

Conclusion

How do you choose suppliers with whom to form long-term partnerships? Now that we've discussed some of the attributes that need to be considered when choosing a supplier to form a long-term partnership, your next step is to consider whether these attributes apply to your facility and its needs. Most of them likely will apply to you, but you may also want to add some or subtract some as you determine your criteria for choosing suppliers to form long-term partnerships. Also, you may want to begin to think about how you are going to get your key players together to discuss the attributes of a good supplier to form a long-term partnership.

Your key players hold valuable information on suppliers, and you'll need to use that information to successfully develop your suppliers into partners. They also likely hold vital expertise on your internal operations. The impact of internal operations on your supply chain and supplier development will be covered in more detail in the next chapter.

INTERNAL OPERATIONS ESSENTIAL TO EXTERNAL SUPPLIER DEVELOPMENT

II

Chapter 5

The Importance of Internal Operations

Introduction

Internal material movement is an early key to effective supplier development.

In this chapter, we'll illustrate the importance of your internal operations, specifically material movement, and its impact on supplier development.

Supplier development can play an important and productive role in a Lean enterprise, but you need to choose the right *time* to focus on supplier development. First, your facility as a whole needs to understand its own Lean production system and the benefits of developing Lean suppliers to support your overall production system.

A Lean Supply Chain Is Built around Solid Core Operations

When we worked with Toyota, we saw something markedly different than we'd seen in other companies: daily mandatory overtime if the target number (Takt time target) of cars to be built was not met. Why did Toyota do this? The practice of working mandatory overtime to meet the target relates to the supply chain and how efficiently material is moved. Mandatory overtime provides stability for the supply chain. Toyota chooses to measure itself on perfection, loading its operators with the exact amount of work needed to make a specific number of cars every day. Because it is very difficult to ever achieve perfection, it is likely that overtime will be needed every day to make the required production number.

For our purposes, the discussion of supplier development, the practice of working mandatory overtime to meet the target relates to the supply chain. While studying the supply chain at Toyota, we noticed one defining characteristic: speed. The velocity at which they move material is astounding, with a near-constant movement of material into and out of the facility. Suppliers deliver components to Toyota on a very frequent basis, often daily, and sometimes even hourly.

The only way that suppliers can deliver product that frequently is if they trust that their customer will pull the quantity of product that they say they will pull, when they say they will. Lacking that trust, a supplier is left to guess whether or not a forecast, created by an antiquated system, is correct. Many times, our operational practices hurt our supply base more than we care to understand.

So why does Toyota require overtime? Toyota works overtime often because if they are scheduled to make 435 cars per shift, they have to make 435 cars per shift. If they do not make 435 cars per shift, there will still be enough parts coming to their facility the next shift to make 435 cars. Their system is built on speed and low inventories in a just-in-time manner. So to protect their supply chain and place less stress on their production system, they choose to work overtime if needed to make the daily production number.

Take the number of suppliers that provide product for the Toyota Production System. Take into account that the entire Lean movement is derived from the Toyota Production System. Now, how would any of the just-in-time philosophy work if the supply base was not given a consistent demand or did not trust that demand? If some days Toyota made 435 cars, some days they made 150 cars, and some days they made 750 cars, how would the supply base run efficiently?

It is very difficult for a supply chain to achieve the possible efficiencies with a customer that is not stable. Internal operations are vital to the effective development of suppliers, as you'll see from the following example.

An Example from Internal Operations

When we discuss supply chains and supplier development, lots of times we will use examples from internal operations, for two reasons. First, many of our clients who are considering supplier development are familiar with Lean operations inside their facilities. This is a very valuable asset. Second, the principles that are used to develop material movement inside the four walls of a facility are the same as they are outside of the facility. As a result, examples from internal operations can help clients better understand external material movement. Take the following example:

Within your Lean production facility, the final assembly line is scheduled to run one hundred pieces of part A, one hundred pieces of part B, and one hundred pieces of part C on Wednesday. If the final assembly line produces a different quantity or mix of part numbers, it causes a problem for the purchasing department. The purchasing department has planned for the final assembly area to produce the specific quantities of one hundred As, one hundred Bs, and one hundred Cs. If final assembly made two hundred instead of the scheduled quantity, purchasing would run out of product because they only planned for one hundred As.

This principle has the same impact on the supplier's effective supplying to the facility. If the supplier is planning to supply one hundred pieces of part A every day in the week, it has planned its production schedules accordingly. It likely will be able to produce the planned number efficiently, but if the customer's facility decides to pull more than that quantity, this will probably cause a disruption in the supplier's production process, which almost always leads to lost money, efficiencies, and time.

On the opposite side of the spectrum, let's look at how the supplier reacts when product is produced according to the schedule. If a supplier can feel confident that its customer is going to pull the quantity of product that they say they are going to pull, the supplier can feel confident in its own production schedule.

Let's look again at our sample schedule: one hundred pieces of part A, one hundred pieces of part B, and one hundred pieces of part C on Wednesday. If the supplier has faith that the customer is going to produce product according to their schedule, then its production will likely be more efficient and cost-effective, which oftentimes leads to a healthier and more competitively priced supplier. This is because the supplier will be able to run with less inventory, manpower, and floor space by making only what product it knows that it needs when it knows that it needs it.

Solid Internal Material Movement Leads to the Knowledge Necessary for Supplier Development

Let's say that throughout the implementation of a Lean production system in a facility, it becomes evident that the way that the facility is receiving its material is not optimal. One of these nonoptimal situations may be in the form of odd box quantities that have no relationship to the finished goods quantity. Say that your finished goods pack-out quantity is one hundred pieces, but you get purchased components that are assembled to that product shipped in a box quantity of seventy-eight pieces. It is kind of like trying to put a square peg in a round hole (Figure 5.1).

In this case, there will always be partial containers in the facility because the quantity of purchased components is not a multiple of the finished goods pack-out quantity. Again, in a supplier-customer relationship where the determining factor is oftentimes piece price cost, the purchased component is sourced to the lowest bidder, who chooses their own shipment quantity. Part of the reason that the part is inexpensive is because of the quantity that it is shipped in. In other words, the quantity of the purchased component is chosen based upon the convenience of the supplier and not the efficiency of the production system of the customer. This situation and its remedy will be discussed in greater detail in Section 4 of this book.

Another side effect of letting the piece price of a purchased component solely drive decision making is that the size of the box that the purchased components are shipped in is determined by the supplier—another example of a decision being made based on the ease of the supplier and not

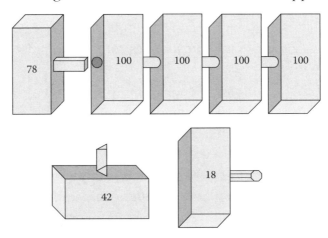

Figure 5.1 Square peg—round hole.

the efficiency of the customers' production system. Allowing the supplier to choose the physical size of the box that the purchased components are shipped in often leads to internal logistical problems in a facility, because every box could be a different size. This makes it very difficult to size delivery racks and supermarkets. In other words, moving a bunch of boxes that are different sizes throughout a production facility is cumbersome and difficult to do in an efficient manner.

As a secondary consideration, this type of thought process in sourcing purchased components is oftentimes not very "green." These components are not likely shipped in returnable containers, but in cardboard boxes, which are either discarded or recycled, and may even take more labor and expense to deal with when everything is included, than returnable containers that are used and then returned to the supplier to be reused.

These are only a few examples of issues you might encounter as you implement a Lean production system. But there is a silver lining: until you get to the stage of Lean production in which your organization can realize the difficulty that these variables are placing on the production system, it likely won't see the need to make a change in the way that it deals with suppliers.

A solid production system is vital to the development of your supply base. When your production facility has been implementing Lean production systems for a long period of time, they will likely understand the need for purchased components to be delivered to them in a multiple of the finished goods pack. They will also begin to see the value in having a standard amount and standard size of containers in your facility. Our goal has always been to have no more than five different standard sizes of containers in a facility and to fill those containers with a quantity of parts that is a multiple of the finished goods pack-out quantity. So, what is your company's containerization philosophy? If you are like many facilities, you don't have one. But a good containerization philosophy, coupled with a good Lean enterprise system, can increase efficiency.

If you can imagine a production facility in which there are only five different sizes of containers, also imagine the ease (compared to your current system of material movement) of having only five sizes of containers in your facility. In this instance, the logistics of moving material both internally and externally are easier and more efficient. We are not saying that every container will be full, but even though some containers may not be full, the efficiencies gained in the logistics of moving the material may far outweigh the inefficiencies of partially filled containers. (Containerization and packaging will be covered in more detail in Chapter 14.)

Conclusion

In this chapter, we've described the importance of solid internal operations and its relationship to supplier development. One of the goals in effectively developing suppliers is to not let piece price cost be the single driving factor that determines where a purchased component is sourced. Without solid and efficient internal Lean production systems, purchased components shipped in a multiple quantity of the finished goods pack-out quantity, purchased components shipped in a standard size container, removal of cardboard, and even sometimes good quality, are not all just good ideas, but important factors that need to be considered when choosing your supplier or suppliers. Solid and efficient Lean production systems, when implemented correctly, put constant pressure on upstream processes to continually improve what they do (Figure 5.2).

A Lean enterprise system is built backwards, unlike a mass production system. In a mass production system, the designer of the system may look at the stamping process first since it is the first process in the system. They will likely try to make that process as efficient as possible. That leads to long runs and very few changeovers. The next step in the process is paint. The designer of the system would likely design the paint department to "efficiently" produce whatever the stamping department gives them. Next, the final assembly department is designed to efficiently produce whatever paint gives them. The entire system is really based around the stamping department, because that was where the system began.

A Lean production system, on the other hand, is built in the opposite direction. A Lean production system begins with the voice of the customer and works its way back upstream. The first question is: What does the customer require? The answer to that question drives the design and development of the final assembly process. The paint process is then designed

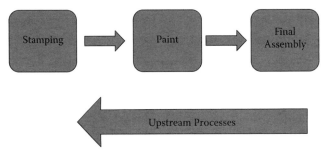

Figure 5.2 Upstream processes.

to support the final assembly department, and the stamping department is designed to support the paint department. In short, the entire Lean production system is designed around the customer's requirements (often referred to as the voice of the customer (VOC)), which were nonexistent in the mass production system design.

If your Lean production system is set up properly, you know that the customer is the one who defines value, and that any Lean enterprise system should be built around providing that value. If your organization has gotten to this point, you most certainly see the need to continue your continuous improvement into the supply base. If your organization is not at that point, we hope that this and previous chapters have illustrated the danger of trying to develop your supply base before you have an efficient production system to support.

The better your internal operations are, the greater the need for Lean supplier development. The better your internal operations are, the greater success rate you will likely have in your Lean supplier development initiatives. And the better your internal operations are, the greater the benefit you will receive in developing your suppliers into partners throughout your Lean supply chain.

Chapter 6

The Plan for Every Part (PFEP)

Introduction

In this chapter, we'll explain what may be the single most important document you'll use as you develop your suppliers into partners: the Plan for Every Part (PFEP). It's a versatile document, and you'll use it to make a number of decisions, both internal and external, for your facility. We'll also explain how to develop your PFEP, and how to use that PFEP to determine what your internal inventory levels should be.

Correctly sizing inventory levels is important, because the correct inventory levels serve as the customer for the supply base. In other words, once your inventory levels are correct, you have a base to support and can set up your supply base to consistently replenish that inventory level. You can also see all of the variables that go into calculating the inventory levels and better understand which decisions need to be made to reduce the inventory levels.

The Need for the Plan for Every Part

As you've already seen in previous chapters, you need a lot of information about the parts in your facility in order to develop suppliers into partners. Through the remainder of this book, we'll refer back to the PFEP for information so that we can effectively develop suppliers to support your Lean enterprise.

For example, we need to know which of the five standard sizes of containers in which we would like to have the product shipped to our facility. The PFEP can provide you with the information needed to make this decision, because it details your part sizes and weights. The PFEP is also important for solidifying internal operations before you begin to develop your suppliers, in that the PFEP can be used to right-size inventory levels within the facility. Many facilities run with much more inventory than they actually need. The PFEP provides the necessary information to size inventories correctly, so that suppliers can then be developed to support those correct inventory levels.

The PFEP

The PFEP is the DNA of your facility, a database that includes information about every part in your facility: purchased components, work-in-process (WIP) parts, and finished goods parts.

You'll recognize much of the information in the PFEP. We're not asking you to make up any information; we just ask you to take the information you already have and put it into a form that you can actually use. Although you already have most of the information that we need for the PFEP, it is likely that you have the information in many different places, and that it is very difficult for multiple people to access. We want a database that is easy to see, sort, and print by anyone in the facility. As material is a large part of many organizations' cost, it is important to have a good understanding of the cost of goods sold (COGS) and other material information. The PFEP will come into play in many different situations throughout the remainder of this book, but we will begin with the quickest bang for your buck: purchased component inventory levels. We will use the PFEP shown in Figure 6.1 throughout this book.

Correct Amount of Inventory

Given the following scenario, how would you respond?

A purchased component has been sourced for your facility, from a supplier in Shanghai, China. The lead time from order to delivery for the component is sixty days. Your facility receives the component every Wednesday at 9:00 a.m. Roughly, what level of inventory should you carry in your facility?

PFEP	6/15/2010		Owner:	Jim Black					
Part #	Description	Avg. Daily Usage (Pcs)	Usage Location	Storage Location	Rack	Position	Section	Shipment Size (Days)	Buffer (Pcs)
14598	Cab	1,000	5D-7-3	Supermarket	A	B3	2	1	500
14579	Hood	1,000	5D-7-4	Supermarket	C	D2	2	5	2,500
14556	Front Frame	1,000	5D-7-5	Supermarket	D	A4	2	60	5,000
14224	Link Nut	4,000	5D-7-6	Supermarket	B	C1	2	5	20,000
14997	Front-End Kit	1,000	5D-7-7	Supermarket	A	B5	2	5	1,000
14448	Back End Kit	1,000	5D-7-8	Supermarket	D	A2	2	120	5,000
10805	Circuit Board	1,000	5D-7-9	Supermarket	E	C3	2	5	5,000

Part #	Buffer (Days)	Transit Time (TT) in Days	Supplier	Supplier City	Supplier State	Country	Container Type	Piece Cost of Component
14598	0.5	1	The Cabby	Georgetown	SC	USA	Expendable	$0.10
14579	2.5	2	J&C INC	Dayton	OH	USA	Returnable	$0.15
14556	5	45	Frames R Us	Shanghai		China	Expendable	$0.75
14224	5	1	S&E Corp.	Charlotte	NC	USA	Returnable	$0.01
14997	1	1	Molding ideas	Asheville	NC	USA	Expendable	$2.00
14448	5	30	Comfy Beds	New Dehli		India	Expendable	$2.00
10805	5	40	PCB Limited	Shanghai		China	Expendable	$2.50

Figure 6.1 The Plan for Every Part.

(Continued)

Part #	Shipment Receiving Day	Reorder Period in Days (RP)	Carrier	Boxes Per Pallet	Supplier Performance Rating	Planned Maximum Inventory	Planned Maximum Inventory in Days	Cost of Planned Maximum Inventory
14598	Daily	1	C&J Freight	NA	1	1,500	1.5	.$150.00
14579	Wed	5	C&J Freight	NA	4	7,500	7.5	$1,125.00
14556	Thur	60	C&J Freight	26	1	65,000	65	$48,750.00
14224	Mon	5	C&J Freight	NA	2	40,000	10	$400.00
14997	Thur	5	C&J Freight	NA	1	6,000	6	$12,000.00
14448	Tue	120	C&J Freight	200	1	125,000	125	$250,000.00
10805	Tue	5	C&J Freight	100	1	10,000	10	$25,000.00

Part #	Box Length (Inches)	Box Width (Inches)	Box Height (Inches)	Usage Per Assembly	Hourly Usage (Pcs)	Pull Quantity (PQ)	Standard Pack (SP)	Standard Packs Used Per Hour	Weight of One Part (Lbs)	Total Package Weight (Lbs)
14598	7	6	6	1	125	100	100	1.25	0.05	5
14579	7	6	6	1	125	100	100	1.25	0.05	6
14556	12	12	12	1	125	5,000	50	2.5	1	51
14224	4	4	4	4	500	20,000	20,000	0.025	0.2	4,001
14997	6	12	6	1	125	100	100	1.25	1	100
14448	12	12	12	1	125	3,000	15	8.33	2	30
10805	3	3	3	1	125	5,000	50	2.5	0.05	2.5

Assumptions: Weekly Delivery = 5 days shipment size; Daily Delivery = 1 day shipment size; Monthly Delivery = 20 days shipment size

Figure 6.1 (Continued) The Plan for Every Part. **(Continued)**

Supplier Performance Scale

Excellent	1
Good	2
Fair	3
Bad	4
Really Bad	5

Figure 6.1 (*Continued*) The Plan for Every Part.

(Daily Usage x Shipment Size) + Purchased Parts
Buffer = Planned Maximum Inventory Level

(DU x SS) + PPB = Planned Maximum Inventory

Figure 6.2 Formula to size purchased inventory levels.

The most common answer we hear when we ask this question of someone implementing Lean enterprise systems is: "At least sixty days, because the lead time is sixty days." However, this isn't necessarily the case; as you will see, there may be a drastic cut in inventory levels when you use the correct inventory formula. The formula for sizing purchased components[*] from your supplier in your purchased parts supermarket is daily usage (DU), multiplied by the shipment size (SS) in days, plus the purchased parts buffer (PPB) in pieces (Figure 6.2).

In essence, what this formula says is that when you receive a shipment of product, you have to have space to store that product, plus your predetermined purchased parts buffer. Remember, the purchased parts supermarket is the single place in the facility where all purchased components are kept.[†] Your purchased parts supermarket will give your organization control over all of the purchased components in the facility because the components can only be in the supermarket, on the delivery route, or at the point of production. Therefore, taking the time to develop a purchased parts supermarket with correct inventory levels can provide stability and a base for the

---

[*] Harris, R., C. Harris, and E. Wilson, **Making Materials Flow** (Cambridge, MA: Lean Enterprise Institute, 2003), 27.

[†] Harris, R., C. Harris, and E. Wilson, **Making Materials Flow** (Cambridge, MA: Lean Enterprise Institute, 2003).

internal material movement system, as well as a starting point for supplier development.

The Purchased Parts Supermarket Buffer

The PFEP contains the information necessary to correctly size the inventory levels in the purchased goods supermarket and the purchase parts supermarket buffer. A purchased parts market buffer is a level of inventory that an organization carries to protect itself from inefficiencies within the system. In other words, the buffer is the level of insurance in the purchased parts supermarket that you are willing to pay for; you are carrying the inventory to ensure that you will run at a higher level of uptime. This is one of those situations where we realize that this extra inventory is waste, but that it is in the system for a specific purpose: to protect you from running out of parts.

The following questions are things that you may want to consider as you size your purchased parts market buffer. Though it is acceptable to use a buffer, in some circumstances, as a practice of good management, make it a rule that you can put a buffer in, but that you must also have a plan to remove the buffer. Without this thought process, you will always be carrying the buffer, whether or not the original rationale for it is still valid. Furthermore, without a *plan* to remove the buffer, there will likely be a lack of pressure to fix the problems that caused the *need* for a supermarket buffer.

Determining the Supermarket Buffer

How Often Do You Receive Material?

The frequency with which you receive material can impact the amount of buffer that you need to carry. If you receive material on a daily basis, then you can likely carry fewer inventories because there is more material being delivered the next day.

On the opposite side of the spectrum, if you receive the material once every six months, then you may have to carry more inventories because the impact of a delayed or low-quality shipment is greater. If the shipment is three or four days late, or the quality of the parts is suspect, then the plant is going to be out of parts for some period of time, whether until the next scheduled shipment or the time that it takes to get an expedited air shipment into the facility.

What Is the Supplier's Quality History?

At one facility, engineers for a specific part got together with a supplier and designed a component. What this meant was that this particular supplier was the only supplier in the world that made that component, which also meant that it was the only supplier where we could purchase the component. The component was a difficult one for the supplier to produce, and only 50% of the products they produced were of sufficient quality for the facility, which meant that the facility had to carry a buffer of double what it was actually supposed to use.

This example underscores the need for a plan to remove the buffer. In our previous example, the buffer carried is justified because it is the only way that the production area will be able to produce product and not run out of parts. However, if there is no plan in place to remove this buffer, there may be a corresponding lack of pressure to help the suppliers improve their quality.

What Is the Supplier's On-Time Performance?

Let's say that a supplier's delivery is rated around 95% on time, plus or minus two days. Although the 95% on-time delivery looks good, for inventory planning purposes, it means that your organization must carry more days of inventory than originally planned to protect itself.

Based on this supplier's on-time performance, your facility will need an extra two days of purchased parts buffer in the market. It's a common scenario, and having this information may provide the necessary pressure to develop more control of the receiving process of product into the facility.

Is the Transportation Method Reliable?

Transportation method reliability is often a reason for a fluctuating inventory level. For example, if your organization is in the Northeast, you may want to carry an extra day of inventory during the winter months. But as always, if you do not have a plan to remove the inventory, you may be carrying an extra day's worth of inventory for snowy roads in the summer.

If parts are brought in from other countries, are there customs issues? Are there issues with travel by sea? Are there issues with travel by railroad? These are certainly not all of the questions that can be asked, but the general thought process might help to determine what level of risk you need to plan for, based on the reliability of the transportation method.

What Is the Physical Distance to the Supplier?

How far are your suppliers from you? The distance between your facility and your supplier's can have an impact on the level of inventory that you need to carry. If a supplier is across the street, it should be easier to get product than if your supplier is across the world.

Does it make sense for you to carry more inventories if your supplier is in another country? The answer to this question may vary on a part-by-part basis, but the question certainly has merit. How much inventory do you need to purchase to guard against your supplier being so far away?

Have the Areas Using This Component Been Level Scheduled?

How your organization produces product can also have a big impact on your inventory levels. For example, if your production department is scheduled to run a level schedule of one hundred pieces of part A, one hundred pieces of part B, and one hundred pieces of part C every day of the week, and they actually run those parts, then you can plan to support that run. However, if the production area decides to produce three hundred pieces of part A in one day, then that places a great deal of pressure on the rest of the system because it goes against the original plan.

If this type of production is common, then the materials department will likely have to plan to carry a much larger inventory to compensate for the lack of prior knowledge regarding what the production department will run on any given day. When the materials department, or any upstream department for that matter, cannot anticipate or trust in what the downstream departments are going to do, they often carry large inventories to keep those departments from running out of product. In short, if you don't control the quantity and mix of part numbers produced, inventory levels will likely be higher.

Correctly Sizing Purchased Component Inventory

Let's use our method of sizing purchased component inventory (DU × SS) + PPB to calculate the purchased component inventory level for all of the parts on our PFEP. The suppliers on our PFEP are fictional and do not represent any real suppliers. Our fictional company is based in Charleston, South Carolina, and assembles toy trucks on a five-day workweek. This information will be utilized throughout the remaining chapters of this book.

Part Number 14598

The first part is the cab, part number 14598. The part is purchased from a company in Georgetown, South Carolina. The daily usage of the component is 1,000 pieces, and the cab is received on a daily basis, so the shipment size is one day (1,000 pieces × shipment size of 1) + purchased parts buffer.

    The supplier for this component has a supplier performance rating of 1, or excellent. Their deliveries are on time, 99% of the time. They are located less than 60 miles from the facility. Their quality has been nearly perfect for the past five years. The supplier also carries a small amount of finished goods inventory, so there does not appear to be a need to carry a large supermarket buffer. Because of their supplier rating and close proximity to the facility, let's assume that we only need a half-day buffer. The half-day buffer will cover us if there's a delay in getting the parts received into our system, a flat tire on a truck, a lot of traffic, etc.

Total maximum inventory level for part number 14598: (1,000 × 1) + 500 = 1,500 pieces, or 1.5 days

Part Number 14579

The hood is part number 14579. Daily usage for the hood is also 1,000 pieces; this component is purchased from a supplier in Dayton, Ohio, which is over 600 miles away. The product is received weekly, so the shipment size is five days: (1,000 pieces × shipment size of 5) + purchased parts buffer.

    This supplier has a supplier performance rating of 4, which is not very good. This supplier has problems both with on-time delivery—they're on time only 50% of the time—and quality. If we allow them a margin of plus or minus two days on their delivery, then their on-time rating rises to 99%. Their quality problems cover a wide range of issues, but we are confident that they have about 10% fallout; in other words, 10% of the product that we receive from this supplier is defective. So, the supermarket buffer for this particular component is two days for the delivery issue and a half day to cover the 10% quality problem, along with the same kinds of little mishaps that could hit any supplier (trouble getting the parts received into our system, a flat tire on a truck, a lot of traffic, etc.).

Total maximum inventory level for part number 14579:
$(1,000 \times 5) + 2,500 = 7,500$ pieces, or 7.5 days

Part Number 14556

The front frame is part number 14556. It is purchased in China, thousands of miles away. The daily usage of this component is, again, one thousand pieces, but the component is only delivered every three months in a shipment size of sixty days, based on twenty workdays per month. For part number 14556, the shipment size is sixty days: (1,000 pieces × shipment size of 60) + purchased parts buffer.

The supplier of this part has a supplier performance rating of 1, which again means that they are an exceptional supplier; they are normally on time and provide a good quality component. However, the supplier is a long way away, and that could cause big problems for production if the supplier ever did have a quality problem. Therefore, we decided to carry an extra five days of inventory as a supermarket buffer; if necessary, we could get product from the supplier to our facility via air shipment within this timeframe. We also have to allow for problems at the border, customs, etc. Also, this supplier does carry a finished goods inventory, so we can get the parts in a hurry if we need them. The amount of supermarket buffer guards against a delay in the shipment. A delay is certainly possible, since the shipment comes by ship to the West Coast, has to pass through customs, and then is put on a train; so five days is the minimum supermarket buffer that we can risk.

Total maximum inventory level for part number 14556:
$(1,000 \times 60) + 5,000 = 65,000$ pieces, or 65 days

Part Number 14224

Part number 14224 is a different kind of part. As you can see by looking at the PFEP, this link nut has a higher daily usage than any other part. This part is also the least expensive part on the PFEP. The standard pack quantity of the part number is twenty thousand pieces, or a week's worth of product. In cases like this, where we are looking at an inexpensive part that is a commodity, we will handle it a little differently. The same methodology of determining the maximum level of inventory holds true, but we may make changes as we look at the situation in more detail.

The part is purchased from a supplier in Charlotte, North Carolina, about 200 miles away. The daily usage for the part is four thousand pieces, and the shipment size is five days because we get a weekly shipment of link nuts from this supplier: (4,000 × shipment size of 5) + purchased parts buffer.

In this case, we can calculate the supermarket buffer a little differently. The supplier performance rating is 2, which is good. They usually send product on time, but sometimes are a little late; the majority of the time their quality is good. When they do have a quality problem, it is minimal; there has never been a whole box of bad product. Not only do we take a look at how close the supplier is and past quality history, but in this case, we also look at the standard pack quantity. Since this is a commodity and a fairly inexpensive part number, we have decided to keep a whole week's worth of supermarket buffer. This is because it is really inexpensive and the standard box size from the supplier is a week's worth of material.

Total maximum inventory level for part number 14224:
(4,000 × 5) + 20,000 = 40,000 pieces, or 10 days (2 boxes)

Part Number 14997

Part number 14997 is the front-end kit purchased from a supplier in Asheville, North Carolina, approximately 300 miles away. Again, we use one thousand pieces of this component per day. Since we receive it on a weekly basis, the shipment size is five days: (1,000 × shipment size of 5) + purchased parts buffer.

The supermarket buffer is going to be fairly small because the supplier is within a day's drive and its supplier performance rating is 1, or excellent. We feel comfortable with this supplier, as they also carry a finished goods inventory and have been very good to work with in the past. So we'll carry a one-day supermarket buffer; again, since we only get a shipment once a week, we want to protect ourselves against any minor mishaps.

Total maximum inventory level for part number 14997:
(1,000 × 5) + 1,000 = 6,000 pieces, or 6 days

Part Number 14448

Part number 14448 is very similar to part number 14997. This part number is the kit to complete the back end of the toy truck, whereas part number 14997 was the kit to complete the front end of the toy truck. This example will illustrate the level of inventory that must be carried when shipment of the product is very infrequent. The daily usage of this kit is 1,000 pieces, but the shipment size is 120 because of the sourcing agreement overseas. So even before we add a purchased parts buffer, we are looking at a maximum inventory level of 120 days: (1,000 × shipment size of 120) + purchased parts buffer.

The supermarket buffer will have to be at least a week to cover the small things that could happen. This particular supplier does have a supplier performance rating of 1 and has proven to be capable.

Total inventory level for part number 14448:
(1,000 × 120) + 5,000 = 125,000 pieces, or 125 days

You can see from the PFEP that the cost of inventory for the back-end kit is $250,000, and the cost of the front-end kit is $12,000. The piece price cost of each kit is the same; however, you have to carry more than twenty times more inventory for the back-end kit than for the front-end kit.

Part Number 10805

The circuit board is part number 10805. Daily usage for the circuit board is one thousand pieces. This component is purchased from a supplier in Shanghai, China, which is more than 7,000 miles away. The product is received weekly, so the shipment size is five days: (1,000 pieces × shipment size of 5) + purchased parts buffer.

This supplier has a performance rating of 1, which is considered excellent. So, the supermarket buffer for this particular component is based primarily on the distance to the supplier. In this case, the purchased parts buffer is going to be five days, because the company feels that it could expedite product from the supplier in China to its receiving dock within a five-day time period.

Total maximum inventory level for part number 10805:
(1,000 × 5) + 5,000 = 10,000 pieces, or 10 days

Your Actual Inventory Levels

When you begin to take this approach to your own inventory levels, you'll likely see that you are carrying a lot more inventory than you actually need. When organizations use the PFEP to attack inventory levels, levels typically drop dramatically. An important thing to remember is that the PFEP stands for Plan for Every Part. That means that every part needs to be dealt with individually.

You need to understand your inventory levels and the variables that go into those inventory levels before you begin to develop your suppliers. When you understand the variables that go into sizing your inventory levels, you may make different sourcing decisions than you would otherwise.

Conclusion

As you've seen, the PFEP is critical to correctly sizing your inventory. The database will be equally as important as you continue to ask your suppliers to change some of the ways in which they ship your products (container type, quantity, etc.). Again, you need to get your inventory to its correct level before you move to developing suppliers. When your inventory levels are correct, you can help your suppliers build a system to support that level of inventory and the velocity at which the material almost certainly has to move to support the lower inventory levels.

You know that material flow is important—perhaps even more important than you may have believed before implementing your Lean enterprise—and the PFEP plays a critical role in the material flow system. If you use the formula for sizing your purchased component inventory, you'll likely be able to decrease your current inventory levels and increase efficiency. You need stability in your production facility before you begin to develop your suppliers, and correctly sizing your inventory is the first step toward that goal. In Section 3, we'll discuss your next consideration: a true cost model.

THE TRUE COST
MODEL

Chapter 7

True Cost Thought Process

Introduction

At some point in time you'll need to decide whether to develop a current supplier or a new supplier. This decision has traditionally been governed by an in-depth comparison of the piece price between a current supplier and a prospective supplier, but is that all of the information you need?

Should a decision be based on piece price alone? In this section, we will guide you through a selection process to help you determine whether or not moving to a new supplier versus retaining an existing supplier is cost-prohibitive. You can also use this same process to compare suppliers for new parts that you don't currently source. The process that you are about to learn will move you from the limited view of looking at sourcing through piece price alone, to a true cost approach.

In the next chapters, we'll discuss:

- what we mean by true cost,
- the components of true cost, and
- how you can calculate true cost.

Note that when we discuss sourcing a new supplier for a current part, we're assuming that all possible efforts to develop your current supplier as a viable partner have been utilized and have failed. The premise of this book is supplier development, not supplier harassment. If you've provided extensive support to your current supplier and your efforts haven't been fruitful, then seeking a new supplier very well may be warranted. But remember, we're not out to pressure your supplier into unreasonable cost, quality, or delivery goals that have no semblance of a partnership philosophy; these draconian methods are no more than an attempt to bully. If you are not working to create a partnership, then the remaining portions of this book are not for you.

Piece Price versus True Cost

What do we mean by true cost? As we've noted in prior chapters, the piece price of an item—how expensive one supplier's piece price is compared to another's—is typically the driving factor for selection of one supplier over another. We've all been in meetings where piece price savings claims are driving the argument to switch suppliers.

But unfortunately, piece price only tells us a fraction of the cost that is actually borne by your organization when you switch to a new supplier. The piece price only takes into account the price that the supplier is willing to sell the item for; it usually includes the supplier's manufacturing, overhead costs, and profit, but may or may not include things such as the cost, to you the customer, for transportation of the goods to your location, or other concealed costs. We'll discuss these costs in more detail in later chapters.

From this point on, when you evaluate a supplier, we want you to use a true cost methodology. The true cost methodology takes into account other costs; considering the piece price as a part of the equation, but also considering other costs, to give you a more refined look at the item and what it really costs you. In this chapter, we'll first think about why you're sourcing or resourcing a part, and then look at some of the issues that go into making that decision in more detail. Later chapters in this section will describe the true cost methodology in more detail.

Why Are You Sourcing/Resourcing?

Let's first think about why you're making a new sourcing decision. Your reasons can be numerous and diverse. One thing that typically drives a change is that your current supplier just may not be meeting your expectations. These expectations usually revolve around cost, quality, or delivery.

Cost Reduction

We find that one of the primary reasons that companies switch suppliers is because your current supplier's cost may exceed the amount that you are willing to pay, or the costs may have grown beyond an acceptable range. When your organization is trying to achieve some type of a cost savings, you'll first identify or attempt to identify a source that can reduce the cost of the associated item.

Quality Concerns

Your supplier's quality may not meet your agreed-upon quality standards. Quality, or lack thereof, is another major reason that can drive a company to seek a new partner—and for good reason: when a supplier doesn't meet your quality requirements, several wastes can be realized by your organization.

When your supplier doesn't meet its obligations to your organization, rework can grow exponentially. For example, you'll need to sort and move the bad parts that have been introduced into the value stream. You'll see extra motion on the part of the operator when the faulty item is discovered, as he or she will need to sort through the parts to find one that meets the requirements rather than selecting any part randomly and knowing that it is suitable for use. When you're tasked with meeting production goals, waiting for the parts to be reworked and the waiting associated with a line-down situation can be costly and aggravating. And inventory can be affected when the customer has to increase the amount required in the supermarket because of scrap found while processing. These are just some of the wastes that you're subjected to because of poor quality parts from a supplier, and of course, with each of these wastes come additional associated costs (a more in-depth discussion on waste is included in Appendix A).

Delivery Concerns

If your supplier can't provide you with the items you need in a timely manner, you'll likely want to seek a change in partnership. If you can get a quality product at the right price but at the wrong time, does it really lead to a successful supply chain? The answer is a simple but unequivocal no!

We know that cost, quality, and delivery are all important factors required for a successful customer-supplier partnership. If any one of these factors is lacking in any way, you'll likely be driven to look for a new supplier. But there are reasons other than poor performance that can lead you to look for a new supplier. We'll go into these next.

New Products

New products can require parts that have never been produced before, so an entirely new sourcing arrangement is needed. You may choose to source these parts with a past or current supplier, or with a supplier that is completely new to your organization.

When you're sourcing a new supplier or suppliers, you'll need to do a fair amount of due diligence to determine if the prospective suppliers are worthy partners. In Chapter 11, we'll look at selecting a supplier from the true cost standpoint, while Chapter 15 will explain what you need to consider when selecting your first partner.

Dual- or Multisourcing Requirements

It may be beneficial for you to have more than one supplier to provide you with the same parts. This strategy can be necessary if you have multiple manufacturing locations that are spread across many geographic locations; in this instance, you'll likely want to have all suppliers, and supplier-provided material, limited to a certain geographic proximity to the manufacturing location. For example, if you have manufacturing facilities in Europe and in North America that are making the same product, you may decide to have both European and North American suppliers supplying their respective continental facilities rather than receiving the part from just one location. This strategy can reduce inventory and shipping, among other costs, and develop more regionalized partnerships.

Production Capacity Concerns (Over/Under)

Another reason to choose a new supplier is capacity: you may decide to seek a new supplier not because of performance issues (cost, quality, delivery), but because your current supplier does not have the capacity to continue providing the part you need. This could be due to under- or over-capacity at the supplier's location.

In the case of undercapacity, a supplier cannot meet a growing demand experienced by the customer, and the customer may need to look for a new supplier to meet their capacity increase. If the issue is one of overcapacity at the supplier, the supplier may need to use their unutilized capacity to support other customers and may need to ask you to look elsewhere for the supply of materials. In this case you could have become too small for the supplier to support; your drop in demand, or small demand, then makes it too difficult for the supplier to continue to supply to you. It's unusual, but this can and does occur from time to time.

Joint Venture Proposals/Agreements

Let's say that your organization has just established a joint venture with another company, and as part of the new relationship, you've reached a supplier agreement. In this case, you may be required to switch to the joint venture company as a supplier to support the agreement.

Relationships of this sort may not lead to the best piece price or true cost, but the benefits of joint ventures can outweigh these disadvantages. If you find yourself in this situation, you'll want to document why the joint venture decision was made, so that your organization as a whole can understand the reasoning behind the decision.

Conclusion

As we've illustrated in this chapter, an organization's sourcing decisions can be complex and varied, ranging from product quality concerns to needs to reduce costs. When you're selecting a supplier, you need to analyze all costs to the organization. Once you have this information in hand, you can develop and use a true cost methodology. The categories and methodology behind the true cost method are explained in the remainder of this section. The following chapters will lead you through the three categories that make up true cost, how to calculate these costs, and show you how your company can develop a model to calculate your true costs.

Chapter 8

Change Cost

Introduction

Again, when investigating whether to change from one supplier to another, the measure of comparison used most often is piece price. Piece price is simply the cost of an item as expressed by the supplier.

Whether that item is a bolt, widget, liquid, or gas, most items are priced based on a unit of measure that represents that piece. Using piece price alone as a supplier-to-supplier cost comparator is quite dangerous, because it does not give us the total picture of the true cost that will be incurred. To understand the costs incurred by switching to a new supplier, let's first look at the change costs associated with making that switch.

Change Costs

Change costs are the costs incurred due to switching from one supplier to another—in other words, costs that are only realized because a change is being made. A good test to perform when developing your specific list of change costs is to ask the key players within the company: *Would the organization be incurring these costs if a new or different supplier were not being sought?*

How do you account for these costs when you're evaluating the price of the item? Many would say that these are just the costs of conducting business, but remember our question to the key players: Would the organization be incurring these costs if a new or different supplier were not being sought?

Generally, the answer is no, or at least not to the extent that is seen when evaluating or switching to a new supplier. These are legitimate costs, and they need to be accounted for somewhere. So how do you characterize these costs? You could bury them in departmental overhead, but if you want a realistic picture of the true cost, these costs should be reflected in the cost of the item. Some of the various types of change costs that should be considered in your determination of the true cost of change are outlined in the following paragraphs.

Travel Cost

When you're considering a new supplier, you'll need to send various personnel in your organization to visit the new supplier and conduct reviews, audits, and other fact-finding activities prior to and after the selection of a new supplier. These trips are usually conducted by personnel from engineering, quality, purchasing, and production control and logistics (PC&L). These trips can range from a few days at a time to a few weeks, depending upon the item that is procured, and, depending on where your supplier is located, will require lesser or greater travel costs.

Lost Time Cost

The personnel who are traveling to a prospective or recently selected supplier could be doing other things with their time. We know what you're thinking: I'll give you the travel argument, but this is stretching it. Hear us out.

Let's take the concept of opportunity cost. *Opportunity cost* is defined as the value of a product forgone to produce or obtain another product. Consider the employees who are tied up evaluating the prospective or new supplier. Are they doing their normal jobs? Again, you must ask the question: Would the organization be incurring these costs if a new or different supplier were not being sought? If the answer is no, and we suspect that it is, isn't this a valid cost to be considered when examining the cost to change?

Inspection Cost

A new product, or a change from one supplier to another, brings with it the need to inspect the product to determine if it meets your—and your customers'—expectations. These inspections can be conducted by internal sources at your company, by your supplier, or by external sources.

Examples of external sources are third-party sorting/inspections firms, many of which have been established within the last decade to take care of the numerous products and components that have been sourced inside and outside the country. Let's look at both the internal and external inspection categories.

Internal Inspection Costs

The natural desire of most organizations is, yet again, to classify these costs as a cost of doing business and attempt to ignore them. However, this is in fact an added cost of the new source if these costs are not incurred on the parts coming from the current supplier.

These costs can be calculated by taking the time spent by the employee(s) to conduct the inspection, times the wage rate, multiplied by the duration of time that the employee(s) will be conducting the inspection. If we know that:

- the inspection will occur for the first six months of the new sourcing activity
- the cost of wages and benefits of the employee is $24/hr
- each inspection will last 10 min each time a shipment is received
- a shipment is received once a week

we can then calculate the internal inspection cost for part number 14579 (Figure 8.1).

External Inspection Costs

The external inspection cost should be defined as the cost of the negotiated contract with the external inspector. It will likely be based on the number of pieces to be inspected over the negotiated period. Instead of using an internal inspection team, let's have the inspection done at a third-party location with third-party labor. If the same 125,000 pieces are being inspected by a third party over the same six-month period, and the cost of the inspection

Part # 14579 Hood
Labor Cost (Wages & Benefits) = $24/hr
Duration of Inspection = 6 months = 25 weeks
Time to complete 1 inspection = 10 mins
Delivery Frequency = Weekly
Daily Demand = 1,000 pcs
1 inspection per week

$24	1 hr	10 min		$4
hr	60 min	inspection	=	inspection

$4	1 inspection		$.0008
inspection	5,000 pcs	=	pc

$.0008	125,000 pcs		$100.00
pc	Duration	=	Duration

Figure 8.1   Cost for Internal Inspection.

Part #14579 Hood
Contract Cost for duration of Inspection = $1,000
Duration of Inspection = 6 months = 25 weeks
Time to complete 1 inspection = 10 mins
Delivery Frequency = Weekly
Daily Demand = 1,000 pcs
1 inspection per week

$1,000	Duration		$.008
Inspection duration	125,000 pcs	=	pc

Figure 8.2   Cost for External Inspection.

contract is $1,000, then the cost of your external inspection would be $.008/ piece for the same timeframe (Figure 8.2).

Note if the shipping of the parts to and from the third-party inspector is not included in your contract and is instead buried in your freight, then the freight cost should also be added and expressed as a per-piece cost.

Testing Cost

When you're bringing your new supplier online, you may be conducting some testing to verify that the part meets company and customer expectations. As with inspection, the testing can be conducted internally within your organization, or it can occur at an external/independent third-party source. Testing can verify that the part meets the print in form, fit, function, performance, etc., and again, the cost of testing must be accounted for in the cost of the part.

Internal Test Cost

These costs, if incurred, can be calculated in the same way as the costs associated with inspection. If the testing is done internally at your company, again, the associated costs need to be reflected in your true cost, since the testing is only needed because the part is being switched from one supplier to another.

If this testing also occurs on the existing supplier's part, then you'll need to add the costs to the existing supplier's piece price, whether the costs are equal or not. Even if the testing is done on the existing part, the cost has probably not been expressed as a component of the piece price. When comparing the costs of each supplier in a sourcing decision, you need to conduct a fair and even ("apples to apples") comparison.

External Test Cost

These costs, if incurred, are also calculated in the same way as our inspection cost example, where we take the total of the cost for the external supplier and divide the cost across the number of pieces tested. As with the inspection cost, you need to be cognizant of any shipping costs associated with the movement of the parts between your facility and the external testing source, and ensure that this cost is captured and counted.

Print Change Cost

Print change cost can be an unpleasant surprise when switching from a part that is made internally to a part made by an external supplier. Many manufacturing companies have discovered that parts were being made more through generational knowledge rather than from documented prints and specifications associated with the company's internal configuration control system.

You're probably wondering how this happens, and you might be sure that it doesn't happen at your facility. But let's take a look at the following scenario. In our scenario, you have a manufacturing organization that has been in existence for many years. You do not have established standard work, or audits that verify that operations are occurring to a prescribed best practice. Let's say that Joe knows that his machine tends to lose it as far as tolerance goes, but he communicates with Larry, who makes the adjoining part on another machine. Between them, and their adjustments, a functionally sufficient part is created and the assembly of these two pieces does not generate any quality issues. Now let's say that both of these parts are sourced to a pair of new suppliers, Larry's part from supplier A and Joe's part from supplier B. Both suppliers are provided with the latest versions of the prints and specifications held in the document control system. We'd expect that when the prototype parts are produced and inspected, they'll meet the documented requirements. What do you think is discovered? That's right: they don't fit correctly, function as required, or form the part that is needed. Just be aware that there may be adjustments going on behind the scenes in your facility, and that you may in fact find yourself faced with print changes when moving to a new supplier.

If our hypothetical example rings true for you, the cost to change the print so that what is made actually works may need to be included in the true cost model. Let's look at how many changes are anticipated (Figure 8.3).

Part #14579 Hood
Cost per print change = $500
# of prints for part = 8
Print Changes required per print = 2
Daily Demand = 1,000 pcs
Work Days/yr = 250
Annual Usage = 250,000 pcs
2 Print Changes x 8 Prints x $500 = $8,000

$8,000		$.032*
	=	
250,000 pcs		pc

Note: This cost is allocated
to the first year only

Figure 8.3   Cost for Print Changes.

Tooling Cost and Amortization

If the part or component that you're considering sourcing to a new supplier requires tooling, then you need to evaluate the associated tooling and amortization costs, by asking the following questions:

■ Will new tooling be required, or will the existing tooling be transferred to the new supplier?

■ If the existing tooling will be used, how much inventory will be required over the normally carried amount to sustain the operation until the new supplier is at the prescribed run rate?

■ If new tooling is used, what is the cost of the new tooling?

■ Will your company or the supplier own the tooling?

■ Will new tooling be amortized?

■ If the new tooling will be amortized, will the amortization be based on pieces or on time?

■ What is the amount of pieces or time that will be used to calculate the amortization?

■ Will there be any up-front cash contribution associated with the tooling?

When you answer these key questions, you will then have a path to calculate the cost of tooling as it relates to piece price and true cost. Let's take part number 14579 once again and show how the tooling costs can be calculated.

The hood tooling is currently owned by the supplier, so if the part were to go to an alternate source, new tooling would be required. Our toy truck company never liked the fact that the supplier owned the tooling, so they've decided that the new tooling will be owned by the company. The cost of the new tooling is $54,000, which will be amortized over a three-year period. To determine how the new tooling costs would be allocated to the true cost, the company did the following calculation in Figure 8.4.

Inventory Cost

When changing to a new supplier there are two inventory costs that should be considered—Supermarket (SM) Costs and Supplier Loop (SL) Costs. The

Part # 14579 Hood
Cost of new tooling = $54,000
Amortization period = 3 yrs
Daily Demand – 1,000 pcs

Work Days/yr = 250
Annual Usage = 250,000 pcs
Cost of Capital = 12%

Entire $54,000 is financed at the 12% cost of capital rate over the 3 years

Yr 1 Interest	Yr 2 Interest	Yr 3 Interest	Total Interest	Total P&I
$5,624.43	$3,608.11	$1,336.07	$10,568.61	$64,568.61
$18,000.00	$18,000.00	$18,000.00	Amortized Tooling Cost per yr	
$23,624.43	$21,608.11	$19,336.07	Total Amortized per year	
$0.09	$0.09	$0.08	True Cost per piece per year	

Figure 8.4 Cost for Tooling & Amortization.

Supermarket Cost is the cost associated with the amount of inventory that is needed to reach the Planned Maximum Inventory level that was discussed in Chapter 6. The Supplier Loop Cost is the cost associated with the amount of inventory that is needed to maintain "the pipeline" between you and the partner. Calculation of the Supplier Loop is described in Chapter 12. Supplier Loop Cost may or may not be applicable depending on your use of Pay on Pull—which is outlined in the next chapter.

The important thing to remember with both of these types of inventory costs is that they are *one-time* costs due to the need to purchase the new suppliers product to establish your required inventories. These costs are only applied in the first year. The carrying cost of this inventory is discussed in the next chapter.

Conclusion

Before you make the move from one supplier to another, you need to determine and document the extent of the costs associated with the switch. Again, you want to determine the true cost of the part. Change costs will provide you with a piece of the puzzle, but to get the true cost, you'll also need to examine the categories of ongoing and risk costs. We'll discuss both of these in later chapters.

Chapter 9

Ongoing Cost

Introduction

In Chapter 8 we discussed change costs, or costs associated with the initial change from an existing supplier to a new supplier. In this chapter, we will discuss how to identify and calculate ongoing costs.

Ongoing costs are those that you'll bear during the duration of time that the new supplier is providing you with product. Ongoing costs *categories* for a new supplier will be the same categories that you see with your existing supplier, but the expenses *within* each category may differ—sometimes significantly—between your current and proposed suppliers. You'll need to calculate these costs from a common base point so that you have a fair "apples to apples" comparison. Developing a strategy to conduct this fair comparison is paramount, and is especially important when determining ongoing costs.

Supplier Visits

Throughout the tenure of a supplier as a provider of product to your organization, it is customary and prudent for you to visit with the supplier on a regular basis. These visits are intended to ensure that the communications and expectations of both parties are verified, and that there have been no negative changes in the manufacturing conditions and processes. Since this should be a requirement for any existing supplier, it makes sense to hold a prospective supplier to the same requirement.

Chances are that the cost of these routine supplier visits weren't factored into the cost of the part originally (when dealing with an existing part), but instead were just absorbed in the overhead of the organization. Many of the costs that we will discuss in this chapter may have never been considered as part of the piece price. But even if these costs are buried in overhead, we want you to identify them. We don't want you to be lulled, as many are, into just letting costs accumulate within the catch-all called burden. Instead, you need to become familiar with these costs and relate them back to the piece price so that you can compare all costs accordingly.

To accurately compare new and existing suppliers, you need a measure to apply to the supplier visit ongoing cost for fair comparison. If you currently visit the existing supplier three times a year for two days each visit, then, as a minimum, you should use the same factor when you compare the costs that will be associated with visiting the proposed new supplier. Categories that should be evaluated for travel to the supplier are the same as those that are used to create a travel expense report, for example, airline tickets, car rental, hotel, meals, rental car gas, airport parking, cab/shuttle bus charges, exchange rate fees, and entertainment expenses, to name a few. If it costs $200 per trip to visit a supplier that is 50 miles away for two days, but it costs $3,000 per trip to visit an overseas supplier, you have already realized a huge increase in the visit because of the difference in cost associated with each trip. This is laid out in the example for part number 14579 (Figure 9.1).

Repacking

Will you need to repack the material from the new supplier into suitable containers for the operator to use or for the material handler to transport? Repacking, if required, can be done internally or externally; either way, the cost to perform this task must be accounted for in your true cost model.

If the repacking takes place internally, then the labor time and cost associated with the parts must be calculated to determine the price per piece that should be apportioned to the repacking activity. If the repacking is done external to the company, then the cost associated with the repacking contract needs to be examined to determine the associated cost.

Part # 14579 Hood   Work Days/yr = 250
Current Travel Cost = $200/trip   Annual Usage = 250,000 pcs
New Travel Cost = $3,000/trip
Number of trips/year = 3
Avg. Daily Usage = 1,000 pcs

$200	3 trips	Yr		$.0024
trip	yr	250,000 pcs	=	pc

$3,000	3 trips	Yr		$.036
trip	yr	250,000 pcs	=	pc

Figure 9.1   Cost for Trips.

Part # 14579 Hood   Work Days/yr = 250
Labor Cost (Wages & Benefits) = $24/hr   Annual Usage = 250,000 pcs
Shifts = 2 shifts @ 16 hrs/day
Repack Time = 30 min/day
Avg. Daily Usage = 1,000 pcs

$24	Hr	30 min	250 days		$3,000
hr	60 min	day	yr	=	yr

$24	Hr	30 min	250 days	Yr		$.012
hr	60 min	day	yr	250,000 pcs	=	pc

Figure 9.2   Cost for Repacking.

Even though repacking may be incidental, or necessary, it is still waste. If the material arrived from the supplier to the line, cell, or operation ready for the operator, then the repacking would not be necessary, and the waste of material movement could be avoided. Since this can often not be avoided, and it is costing you money, you must account for it (Figure 9.2).

The annual cost of the repacking activity is $3,000, which increases the cost per piece by $0.012. This may not seem like much for a part that has a piece price of $0.75, but a cost is a cost. If there are ten of these costs throughout the ongoing cost category, then the increase would be $0.12 per piece. Again, you might be saying, "Well that's really not much." What if the cost of this item was $0.075 instead of $0.75? Would the cost be lower for the repacking activity? Would the cost now seem much more consequential? Remember, you need to consider every cost, no matter how large or small, and how those costs are and should be allocated to give you a better overall view of your sourcing decision.

Pay-on-Pull and Consignment

Will your parts be on a pay-on-pull or consignment agreement? One thing that you need to consider when looking at changing suppliers is whether the amount of inventory currently carried in the system will increase, decrease, or stay the same. You can determine this, at least in part, by deciding how the parts will be classified both within your facility and when they're in transit to your facility. Whether you have decided to use a pay-on-pull concept from a stock that is within your facility, a facility that you own, or a third-party or supplier's facility, you need to determine the amount of inventory that you own and the costs associated with it. You also need to consider the point at which the material is transferred to your books. Pay-on-pull and consignment concepts can relieve the effects of a possible increase in inventory within a supply chain.

Pay-on-pull and consigned inventories are normally associated with an amount of inventory that is kept either in the customer's facility or in a facility nearby. This inventory is typically not placed on the customer's books or received into the customer's inventory until it is pulled from the pay-on-pull location. In essence, pulling the material acts as a release against a purchase order so a payable is generated. The amount of pay-on-pull inventory will vary depending on the arrangements that are made between the supplier and the customer. The amount can also vary greatly depending on the physical distance from the supplier to the customer, ranging from a few hours' worth of inventory to several weeks' worth, depending on the replenishment cycle and agreed-upon buffers.

If the amount of inventory held on a pay-on-pull agreement is increased, you won't incur additional costs from a piece price point of view, but the physical space needed to store the material still has a cost. The cost associated with this space is an opportunity cost, since you could use this space to store other materials or to manufacture products. The cost of this space can be applied by determining the cost associated with maintaining a square foot of space (your facility cost) and determining a price per piece for the space being used to house the pay-on-pull material.

Inventory Change

Depending on whether you use pay-on-pull, consignment, or none of these, the change in inventory that accompanies a change in supplier can be significant. Whether this change increases or decreases your cost is a function of the amount of the change in inventory, the price per piece, and the cost of capital to your company.

If your company does not use a pay-on-pull or consignment system, a cost change is likely when you switch to a new supplier, and you'll need to calculate whether this cost is higher or lower than your current inventory cost. You'll recall that in Chapter 6, we defined the calculation to determine the planned max inventory of a part:

Planned max inventory =
(Daily usage × shipment size in days) + purchased parts buffer* in pieces

In Chapter 12, we will describe the calculation to determine how many pull signals you and your partner should use. For now, we'll just discuss the calculation.

To determine the inventory cost of a proposed change, let's take a look at the following two examples. In the first example, we'll examine the inventory for a supplier on a pay-on-pull arrangement.

For our second example, we'll look at the same supplier, but in this case, the supplier won't be on the pay-on-pull relationship with the customer. The information for the calculation is taken from the PFEP for part number 10805. The amount of inventory that is required in the supermarket and number of pull signals in the loop for the pay-on-pull example is shown in Figure 9.3.

The supermarket calculation shows that the planned maximum inventory for the market is ten thousand pieces; this is the number that the company

---

* Harris, R., C. Harris, and E. Wilson, **Making Materials Flow—A Lean Material-Handling Guide for Operations, Production-Control, and Engineering Professionals** (Cambridge MA: The Lean Enterprise Institute, 2003).

Part # 10805 Circuit Board
Avg. Daily Usage = 1,000 pcs
Reorder Period (RP) = Weekly
Shipment Size = 5 days
Ship Frequency = Weekly
Work Days/yr = 250
Cost of Capital = 12%

Transit Time (TT) = 40 days
Piece Price = $2.50
Standard Pack (SP) = 50 pcs
Pull Quantity (PQ) = 1 pallet = 5,000 pcs
Purchased Parts Buffer (PPB) = 5 days
Partner's Time to Replenish (PTR) = 5 days

Planned Max Inventory = (Daily Demand X Shipment Size in Days) + Purchased Parts Buffer in Pcs

1,000 x 5 days + 5,000 pcs = 10,000 pcs
# of Pull Signals in Loop = 11 Pull Signals

Figure 9.3   Planned Max Inventory.

uses for planning purposes. There are 11 pull signals, or 11 pallets (totaling 55,000 pieces), in the loop between the supplier and the customer at any given time. The calculation for determining the number of pull signals in the loop is covered in Chapter 12. This might seem like an excessive amount of inventory, but it is the amount that is required in the "pipeline" to supply the customer's demand of five thousand pieces a week.

Now that we know the amount of inventory planned for the supermarket, we can calculate the cost of the inventory. The pay-on-pull arrangement between the supplier and the customer states that the customer owns the entire inventory that is at their facility and there is no liability for the material that is in transit and has not arrived at the customer's facility. If there was a liability arrangement, then that cost should also be allocated to the inventory cost. The inventory cost for the planned maximum inventory in this example is $28,000 per year (includes cost of capital), for a true cost per piece of $0.112 per year (Figure 9.4).

In Figure 9.4, pay-on-pull has been instituted and the inventory in transit is owned by the supplier. We define *inventory in transit* as *all* of the pull signals that are in transit to the customer; it does not, however, include any signals that the supplier has received from the customer and is in the process of replenishing. The cost of capital must be applied to get the actual cost of the inventory. The cost of capital to the company was discussed previously when we calculated the tooling amortization. The current cost of capital that the company is using is 12%; they can use this information to calculate the costs associated with their inventory.

Cost of Planned Max Inventory: 10,000 pcs x $2.50 pc = $25,000

Planned Max Inventory Carrying Cost: $25,000 x 12% = $3,000

$25,000	Yr		$0.10
yr	250,000 pcs	=	pc

$3,000	Yr		$.012
yr	250,000 pcs	=	pc

True Cost of Inventory: $25,000 + $3,000 = $28,000/yr

Inventory True Cost per year = $0.112 per piece

Figure 9.4   True Cost of Inventory.

The total inventory cost includes the annual carrying and material costs; as noted previously, for the most complete total cost, the cost of the square footage used to store the material can also be calculated. In this case, the company has decided not to include material storage for any current or future supplier. Since the inventory cost was never included in the original piece price provided by the supplier, the $0.112 per piece cost, or 4.48% increase, has been buried. But, what if the supplier was not on a pay-on-pull agreement with the customer? What would the inventory costs look like in this case?

If the supplier is not on pay-on-pull, a significant amount of cost needs to be added to the piece price. This additional cost comes from the planned maximum inventory and the inventory in transit in the loop between the supplier and the customer. The pay-on-pull or consignment relationship between the customer and the supplier does not put any of the material into the company's inventory (rather, material is billed as it is used), but most other relationships are not like pay-on-pull. In our scenario, the inventory costs will be calculated and included in the piece price (Figure 9.5).

Number of Pieces in the Loop: 11 pull signals x 5000 pcs/pull signal = 55,000 pcs
Customer Owned Inventory in Loop = (Pieces in Loop) x Transit %
55,000 pcs x 95% = 52,250 pcs

Figure 9.5   Number of Pieces in the Loop.

Cost of Customer Owned Inventory in Loop: 52,250 pcs x $2.50/pc = $130,625

Carrying Cost of Customer Inventory: $130,625 x 12% = $15,675

$130,625	Yr		$0.5225
yr	250,000 pcs	=	pc

$15,675	Yr		$0.0627
yr	250,000 pcs	=	pc

True Cost of Inventory: $130,625 + $15,675 = $146,300/yr

Inventory True Cost per Year = $0.5852 per piece

Figure 9.6   True Cost of Inventory.

To calculate the total inventory owned by the customer, we need to allot a percentage of the total loop as in transit. Historically, the company sees approximately 90% to 95% of the total loop in the inventory at the plant and as inventory in transit; the remaining 5% to 10% are pull signals not yet ordered (for example, between order periods) or which are being processed at the supplier's location. Because of this, there are approximately 52,250 pieces of additional material that would be owned by the customer and on the customer's books if they were not using pay-on-pull. The cost of this inventory is calculated the same way as the cost of the pay-on-pull inventory (Figure 9.6).

Just as in our pay-on-pull example, the annual inventory cost is equal to the carrying cost and material cost. And, like the pay-on-pull example, the cost of the square footage used to store the material is not included by the decision of the company and to make the examples comparable. The inventory cost in this example is startling. The original piece price is $2.50. Our pay-on-pull example yielded a $0.112 per piece, or 4.48%, increase, while in this example, we have a $0.5852 per piece, or 23.4%, increase.

Freight

The cost to ship products from a supplier's location to your location can be, and in most cases is, priced into the quoted piece price of the part. If the cost is not figured into the piece price of the existing or prospective supplier, you'll need to add it to your calculations.

This is especially important when you have shipments coming from different regions, domestic and foreign. An item that is shipped from a supplier 20 miles vs. 200 miles vs. 6,000 miles away can have grossly different costs. The difference in these costs can make a projected savings of one supplier over the other disappear in a matter of just a few computer keystrokes. You can avoid this by developing a matrix of shipping costs, so that in investigating a sourcing decision you can quickly determine how much an item would cost if shipped from an assortment of possible domestic and foreign locations. The matrix should include air, ground, and sea options. An example of such a matrix is included in Figure 9.7.

Cross-Docking

Cross-docking is the practice of moving goods in a transfer facility from receiving to shipping as quickly as possible. Cross-docking is frequently used when products are brought into the facility via various transportation modes and then must be quickly rerouted to customers.

This practice attempts to minimize the amount of time that goods wait in a traditional warehouse by rapidly consolidating and forwarding multiple vendor shipments to the customer. If you use cross-docking, you need to express it in the determination of the true cost. As freight, this cost is particularly vulnerable to being buried in overhead, but again, to determine your true cost, you need to incorporate freight into your piece price. If your cross-docking facility is used for an assortment of parts, then that cost should be allocated across those parts and apportioned per piece.

Customs and Duties

Many products entering the country from foreign suppliers are subject to duties and required to clear customs. Once you determine whether duties apply, you can calculate the cost of the duties and apply them to your piece price.

Mode	METHOD/FROM	USA Midwest	USA South	USA Northeast	USA West	Mexico	Canada	Europe	South America	India	China
Air LTL 10	Air < 10 Lbs	99	88	107	116	66	149	264	172	91	197
Air LTL 100	100 lbs > Air => 10 Lbs	400	400	426	475	316	399	625	804	511	1,162
Air LTL 1000	1,000 >= Air => 100 Lbs	1,685	1,685	1,955	3,405	830	2,600	1,170	1,690	1,700	1,670
Sea LCL 10	Sea < 10 Lbs							1,500	1,175	1,768	1,250
Sea LCL 100	100 lbs > Sea => 10 Lbs							1,500	1,175	1,768	1,250
Sea LCL 1000	1,000 lbs >= Sea => 100 Lbs							1,500	1,175	1,768	1,250
Sea FCL 20'	Sea 20' Container							1,500	1,75	1,768	1,250
Sea FCL 40'	Sea 40' Container							1,500	1,175	1,768	1,500
Sea FCL 40' HQ	Sea 40' HQ Container							1,500	1,175	1,768	1,500
Truck LTL 10	Truck < 10 Lbs	15	7	15	17	66	23				
Truck LTL 100	100 lbs > Truck => 10 Lbs	73	72	78	94	316	109				
Truck LTL 1000	1,000 lbs >= Truck => 100 Lbs	670	300	320	605	405	425				
Truck Load	Truck 53'	700	700	700	900	1,150	800				

Figure 9.7 Shipping Matrix.

Conclusion

Don't overlook ongoing costs when you're determining the true cost of a part. Often, some of these costs are typically buried in overhead and never applied to the piece price, but again, to get to the true cost, you need to calculate *all* costs. The last cost category we'll cover before we build a true cost model is risk cost. We'll talk more about risk cost in Chapter 10.

Chapter 10

Risk Cost

Introduction

Whether your prospective supplier is 20 miles or 6,500 miles away, you run a risk any time you make a change. Your current supplier knows you and you know them. You've established a certain rapport, whether good or bad, and there's a degree of mutual knowledge between you, the customer, and your supplier.

Even if your prospective supplier is part of your current supplier base, they may have never supplied you with this particular item before. It is because of this new relationship that a certain risk surrounds any move from one supplier to another. The good news is that you can reasonably project and establish a risk cost *before* making a new supplier decision.

Risk Costs

What's a risk cost? It's not a given, but it's a cost that we *can reasonably predict could occur in the course of doing business with a supplier.* Ask around, and you'll find that anyone in manufacturing, especially those working within procurement and supply chain management, can tell you a horror story about a botched change-over of suppliers. These stories are infamous, and only funny in retrospect. Don't add yours to the list.

Every change runs these risks. Every change is susceptible to these mis-steps. It's true that risk costs are not as concrete as change costs or ongoing costs, but we need to expect—and plan for—the unexpected.

If you approach this seriously, you can come up with, and reach consensus on, an organizational list of risk costs. The following common risk costs can act as a foundation for your discussion; although this list is by no means exhaustive, it contains examples from our combined knowledge.

Sorting (Spill Cost)

Do you have a quality role in your organization? Although we are all responsible for quality, undoubtedly there is a quality assurance, quality control, quality inspector, quality manager, VP of quality, or quality network (you get the idea) in your company.

Have you ever heard someone in this type of organization say that there is a "spill" at one of your suppliers? In some cases this is a literal spill, but in most cases a spill refers to a supplier problem that requires immediate action, similar to action that would be taken if something were spilled on the floor. There can be many costs associated with a spill and containing the spill, the first of which is sorting the suspect items.

Who's going to sort these items? In a perfect world, if the supplier is responsible for the spill, the supplier will take responsibility for the sorting, and if your supplier is local, they may be able to send personnel to your facility to sort. If distance and timing don't allow this, however, then your personnel or a third party may need to handle the sorting. Lest we forget our dependence upon the pull signals in the loop, there may also be parts in transit that will need to be sorted when they arrive. Of course, this assumes that sorting is even possible; if the spilled item is not a physical part, but rather a liquid component or compound, then the part may need to be scrapped.

When you're calculating risk costs for a spill, you need to consider not only the likelihood and possible frequency of spills, but also the timeframe necessary to correct the spill and get the situation under control. This timeframe could be five, fifteen, or thirty days or more, but you need to establish as specific a timeframe as possible, which in turn allows you to estimate a cost that can be converted to a cost per piece.

Emergency Travel

When a spill occurs, you'll likely need to send personnel to the supplier to ascertain the extent and severity of the situation and develop a plan to get back on track. Use the same methodology to calculate risk travel costs as you do to calculate change travel costs. Estimate the designated number of trips needed to bring the issue to resolution, and use that estimate as a standard to apply to all sourcing evaluations in the future.

Lost Time

This is the lost time experienced by the person having to do the emergency travel, and again, it's similar to the lost time costs we've seen in the change and ongoing costs categories. Since we know that spills do occur, we can anticipate that someone from the organization will travel to the supplier to ensure prompt correction of the incident; this person's time should be accounted for in your risk cost calculations.

Expediting

Expediting costs are associated with the efforts that it will take to get parts from the supplier to replace the unacceptable material. Remember, this includes the material that is both in your facility and in transit.

Expediting can be extremely expensive, and hopefully you find this method of material movement extremely uncommon. But once again, it is usually very common when a facility is dealing with a spill.

Conclusion

Risk costs are costs that you hopefully will never see but are likely to experience. It may be difficult for an organization to look at these costs as valid, but if you anticipate and add them to each supplier evaluation, then the same standard can be applied.

In the next chapter, we'll show you each of the cost categories, and how to use them to establish a model that your organization can use to calculate and document the true cost of a part.

Chapter 11

True Cost Sourcing

Introduction

In this chapter, we'll take you through some examples of sourcing decisions, including a strict piece price comparison and the same comparison made using a true cost model.

The true cost model described in the following pages will show you how to use the different types of costs we've discussed in previous chapters to create a tool that you can use to effectively compare suppliers and determine a realistic cost per piece. The three examples in this chapter will compare suppliers who provide the same part. To help you understand how to develop and use a true cost model, we have created a model that includes the categories and concepts discussed in the preceding chapters. The model is not all-inclusive, but it will allow you to visualize how your data can be compiled and presented. The remainder of this chapter will walk you through the modeling process.

Building the Model

In order to more efficiently evaluate your suppliers and properly obtain a true cost, you need to build a model that is easy to use and that will allow for standardized input and presentation of data. Just as the Plan for Every Part (PFEP) should be built inside of a spreadsheet or database, a true cost model should also be created in a spreadsheet or database available for use across the organization.

The model will be the means to collect, calculate, and depict all aspects of how a supplier provides a part, and should be put into a format that can be quickly used to compare the same part as provided by different suppliers. The model should consist of five basic components:

1. Part and supplier data
2. Change cost inputs
3. Ongoing cost inputs
4. Risk cost inputs
5. Graphical results

Part and Supplier Data

Part and supplier data information can be found in the PFEP and provided by members of the materials and finance groups within your organization. The data required creates the foundation for many of the calculations that are necessary in the model (Figure 11.1). Part and supplier data should also answer three key questions:

Is this the current supplier? If the supplier in question is currently providing you with the part, there are certain costs that will not be calculated or included in the model—primarily change costs.

In addition, if the model is being generated to compare the current supplier of a part to a prospective supplier, the distinction between suppliers will be clear to all.

Is freight included in the quoted piece price? In other words, is the transportation price of the part treated as a distinct element of the piece price, or is it hidden in overhead? If freight is included, then you do not want to double count it when calculating ongoing costs.

Conversely, if the freight has not been included, you don't want to overlook it as a component. The cost of freight can be significant, as we'll show later.

Are customs and duties included in the piece price? If customs and duties charges are required for the part, you'll need to make a distinction as to whether the costs are quoted in the piece price or are separate.

| Part # | 14579 | Description: | Hood | Supplier Name: | J&C Inc. | Current/Proposed Supplier Location: | USA - Midwest ▼ | Using Location: | USA - South ▼ |

Is This the Current Supplier? ⦿ YES ○ NO   Is Freight Included in the Quoted Piece Price? ⦿ YES ○ NO   Are Customs & Duties Included in Piece Price? ○ YES ⦿ NO

Quoted Piece Price	$0.15	Annual Usage	250,000	Workdays/Year	250	Workdays/Week	5
Cost of Capital	12%	Part Weight (lbs)	0.05	Avg. Weekly Usage	5,000	Avg. Daily Usage	1,000
Shipment Size in Days	5	Partners Time to Replenish (days)	14	Reorder Period (days)	5	Transit Time (TT) (days)	2
Pull Qty (pcs)	100	Purchased Parts Buffer (days)	2.5				

Figure 11.1 Part and Supplier Data Input.

If there are customs and duties charges on a part, these charges can be buried in overhead, not unlike what we can see with freight. Again, the answer to this question will have an impact on the ongoing cost.

Cost of Capital (Cost of Debt)

Since most companies carry some type of debt, your finance department will need to supply you with a cost-of-capital input. This percentage is calculated differently by different organizations. Although cost of capital isn't the focus of your true cost model, we can't overlook it; we need to identify, document, and apply that percentage to your modeling process to arrive at a true cost.

Change Cost Inputs

In Chapter 8, we discussed several inputs to the change cost category (Figure 11.2).

Part number 14579 is currently being procured from J&C, Inc., as indicated in the part and supplier data section of the model shown in Figure 11.1. Since J&C, Inc. is the current supplier, there are no change costs reflected in the model, but we still want to show all of the associated fields. In the following pages, we will break down each section of the change cost inputs section illustrated in Figure 11.2. Examples of proposed suppliers will be shown later in this chapter.

Travel and Lost Time Cost

For our model, we're estimating separate one-week trips. A matrix of ten regions was created to help quickly look up travel costs. Based on this projected number of trips to suppliers, we'll calculate our travel costs to the supplier for our first year.

Our human resources department has estimated an average weekly salary for the organizations that typically travel in support of supplier part procurement and sustainment (purchasing, quality, engineering, etc.). We'll also calculate lost time costs for our anticipated trips (identified as number of trips per year) (Figure 11.3).

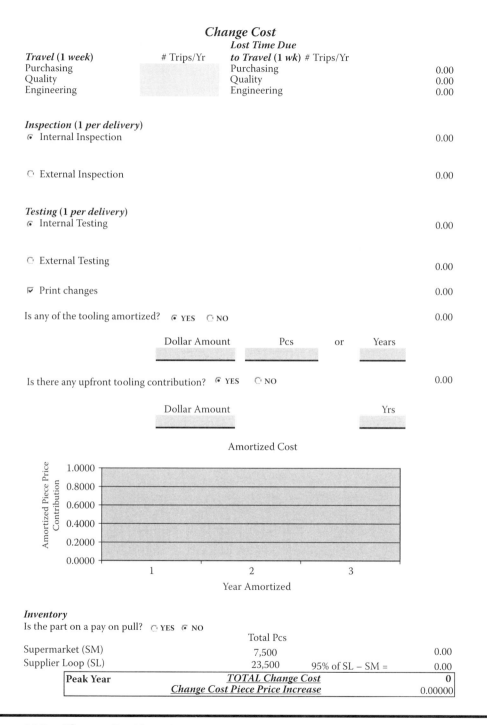

Change Cost

Travel (**1 week**)	# Trips/Yr	*Lost Time Due to Travel* (**1 wk**)	# Trips/Yr	
Purchasing		Purchasing		0.00
Quality		Quality		0.00
Engineering		Engineering		0.00

Inspection (**1 per delivery**)

⊙ Internal Inspection ... 0.00

○ External Inspection ... 0.00

Testing (**1 per delivery**)

⊙ Internal Testing ... 0.00

○ External Testing ... 0.00

☑ Print changes ... 0.00

Is any of the tooling amortized? ⊙ YES ○ NO ... 0.00

Dollar Amount	Pcs	or	Years

Is there any upfront tooling contribution? ⊙ YES ○ NO ... 0.00

Dollar Amount	Yrs

Amortized Cost

Inventory

Is the part on a pay on pull? ○ YES ⊙ NO

	Total Pcs		
Supermarket (SM)	7,500		0.00
Supplier Loop (SL)	23,500	95% of SL – SM =	0.00

Peak Year	*TOTAL Change Cost*	**0**
	Change Cost Piece Price Increase	0.00000

Figure 11.2 Change Cost Input.

Travel (1 week)	# Trips/Yr	Lost Time Due to Travel (1 wk)	# Trips/Yr
Purchasing		Purchasing	0.00
Quality		Quality	0.00
Engineering		Engineering	0.00

Figure 11.3   Travel & Lost Time Cost Inputs.

Inspection and Testing

In our inspection and testing categories, we'll calculate the costs associated with initial incoming inspection and surveillance testing that are typically experienced within the first year and the timeframe prior to initial delivery. Separate calculation areas were created to calculate internal and external testing and inspection. The calculation is based on one inspection occurring per delivery, and the part and supplier information at the top of the model (Figure 11.4).

Print Changes

Costs associated with print changes are determined by taking an average print change cost and designating the number of anticipated print changes.

Tooling and Tooling Amortization

In Chapter 8, we discussed tooling and its potential effects as a change cost. In this section of the model, we'll identify whether new tooling will be

Inspection (1 per delivery)	Inspector Wages/Hr	Time to Inspect (mins.)	Duration (Days)	Duration Cost	
Internal Inspection				0.00	0.00
External Inspection					0.00

Testing (1 per delivery)	Tester Wage/hr	Time to Test (mins.)	Duration (Days)	Duration Cost	
Internal Testing				0.00	0.00
External Testing					0.00

Figure 11.4   Inspection and Testing Inputs.

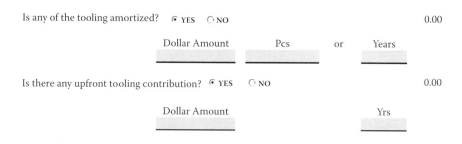

Figure 11.5 Amortized Cost Inputs.

needed and how it will be amortized, with or without any up-front tooling contribution capital.

For our example model, we're allowed no more than three years to amortize tooling and to allocate toward up-front contribution to the tooling. The amortized cost input area is used to calculate the amount of cost per piece that is allocated within a specific year (Figure 11.5).

Inventory

The inventory area in the model identifies whether you're using a pay-on-pull concept and calculates the planned maximum inventory for the supermarket. It also calculates the number of signals in the loop between the supplier and the customer, which we'll discuss in more detail in Chapter 12. Costs associated with the inventory include the cost of capital identified in the part and supplier information data (Figure 11.6).

Ongoing Cost Inputs

The ongoing cost section of the model identifies the costs that are standard to your current supplier and the same costs as identified for a proposed supplier (Figure 11.7). In the following pages, we will examine each section of the ongoing cost portion of the true cost model.

Inventory
Is the part on a pay on pull?   ○ YES   ● NO

	Total Pcs		
Supermarket (SM)	7,500		0.00
Supplier Loop (SL)	23,500	95% of SL – SM	0.00

Figure 11.6 Inventory Inputs.

Travel (1 *week*)	# Trips/Yr	***Ongoing Cost*** *Lost Time Due* ***to Travel*** (1 *wk*)	# Trips/Yr	
		Ongoing Cost		
Purchasing	1	Purchasing	1	2,950.00
Quality	1	Quality	1	2,940.00
Engineering	1	Engineering	1	3,020.00

Repacking	Operator Wages/Hr	Time to Inspect (mins.)	
Internal ▾			0.00

Inventory			
Supermarket Carrying Cost			135.00
Supplier Loop Carrying Cost		95% of SL – SM =	273.60

Freight		
Truck 53' ▾		0.00
Will the part be crossdocked? ○ YES ● NO		0.00
Customs & Duties ○ YES ● NO		0.00

Peak Year	*TOTAL Ongoing Cost*	$	9,319
	Ongoing Cost Piece Price Increase		0.03727

Figure 11.7   Ongoing Cost Input.

Travel and Lost Time Cost

For the ongoing cost section of the model, we calculate travel and lost time cost in the same way that they are calculated in the change cost section of the model. Again, the basis of the costs in this section is determined by establishing a standard number of trips per year to be taken by purchasing, quality, and engineering.

Repacking

In the repacking section of the model, we can calculate the cost associated with repacking a part from the packaging provided when it arrives at a facility, to packaging that is consistent with the operations of a facility. The costs can be calculated for either internal or external repacking activities (Figure 11.8).

Freight

The freight area in the model calculates the freight costs associated with shipping the part from the supplier to the customer. Several freight options

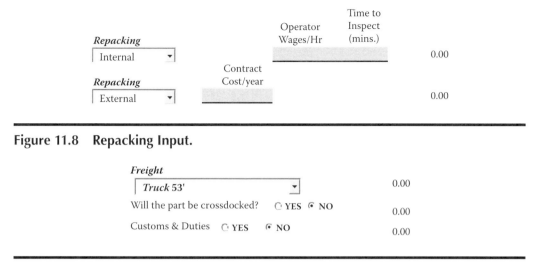

Figure 11.8   Repacking Input.

Figure 11.9   Freight Input.

are provided; we've also created a freight matrix from cross-functional discussions to compare all suppliers. Calculating cross-docking and customs and duties (if not included in piece price) is also contained in the freight section (Figure 11.9).

Risk Cost

The risk cost section incorporates four costs likely to be experienced with any supplier; these risk costs center around the issue associated with a quality spill.

The criterion allows for one spill per year for any supplier evaluated. The differences in cost in this section are calculated based on part and supplier data, along with the information provided in the other sections (Figure 11.10).

Cost Comparison Examples

So far in this chapter, we've discussed the components that make up your true cost model; these components can be used to compare suppliers as needed. The model gives an equal footing to each supplier and allows you to view the costs associated with each supplier without bias. The model also allows the organization conducting the review to get a better picture of the true cost associated with the part and supplier being considered. Let's take a look at three examples of how we can use the model to do this:

Risk Cost	
Sorting Costs per Spill @ $300/day (sort until new stock arrives)	7,050.00
Emergency Travel of 1 week to address spill (Quality Only)	1,400.00
Lost Time of one week during Emergency Travel (Quality Only)	1,540.00
Expedite (Once per year – 1 Shipment of parts)	1,010.10

Peak Year	TOTAL Risk Cost	$11,000
	Risk Cost Piece Price Increase	0.0440

Figure 11.10   Risk Cost Input.

- The evaluation of part number 14579 from a domestic supplier to an overseas supplier
- The evaluation of part number 14224 from one domestic supplier to another domestic supplier
- The evaluation of part number 10805 from an overseas supplier to a domestic supplier

Part Number 14579 Comparison

Figures 11.11 and 11.12 illustrate the data from the current and prospective suppliers, respectively, for part number 14579 and give you an idea of how the cost categories for the piece price versus true cost compare. The piece price quote from the proposed supplier was 17% ($0.025) less than that of the current supplier; with the current projected annual demand of 250,000 pieces, that's a $6,250 annual savings. However, a different picture emerges when we use the true cost model.

Change costs associated with the proposed move will help drive our piece price cost to almost $1.00 in the first year, an *increase* of $0.75 per piece when compared to the true cost of $0.24 per piece for the current supplier. This is primarily the result of the increase in inventory needed to fill the supply chain the first year and tooling. The subsequent years show a true cost for the proposed supplier decreasing and leveling out to about $0.69 per piece, which is better, but still doesn't even approach the projected savings.

When based on price alone, the proposed supplier presents a compelling reason to change. But when measured against the true cost, the supplier does not realize a savings at all; in fact, a change would more than *double* the cost that the facility experiences with the current supplier (Figures 11.11 and 11.12).

Part Number 14224 Comparison

Let's take a look at our next part. In this example, we're comparing the cost of part number 14224 between the current supplier and a prospective supplier from a different region in the country. As Figure 11.13 shows, the current supplier piece price of $0.01 is actually more along the lines of a $0.03 true cost per piece.

But let's take another look at the proposed supplier in Figure 11.14. Although the proposed supplier's piece price is 20% less than the piece price of the current supplier, the true cost is more than ten times the piece price quoted for the first year, and just under nine times in the remaining three years. Why does the true cost model reflect this?

When we review the true cost model, it becomes apparent that buried costs can have a significant impact when revealed. The primary areas that are causing the model to shift are the travel, freight, and repacking cost associated with the proposed supplier. The ongoing cost alone has removed any potential realized savings. Freight is not included in the proposed supplier's piece price, while it is with the current supplier, and must be cost out separately. In addition, repacking cost will be required when the new supplier's parts arrive at the facility, which adds more cost than the current supplier's part.

Part Number 10805 Comparison

In this example the existing supplier is evaluated against a proposed supplier that has a higher piece price. Why even bother with this evaluation since the proposed supplier is not competitive based on piece cost? As you saw in the previous examples, true cost is not necessarily intuitive. The existing supplier has a quoted cost of $2.50 per piece and a true cost of just over $3.02 per piece. The proposed supplier has quoted a price of $2.75 per piece. The proposed supplier's cost is already 10% greater than the existing supplier's piece price. But, when we review the true cost model, it shows that the proposed supplier's true cost is about $2.99 to $2.81 over the four-year evaluation period. This ranges from about 1% to 7% *less* than the current supplier's true cost.

How can this be? If you examine the comparison you will see that there is a significant transportation and inventory decrease with the proposed

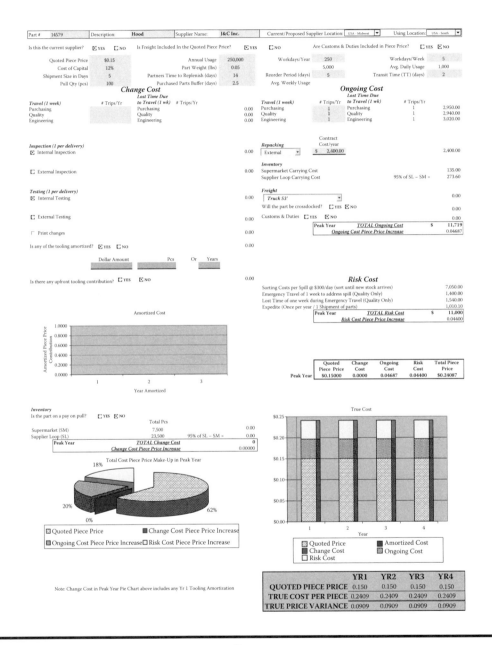

Figure 11.11   Part # 14579 Current Supplier.

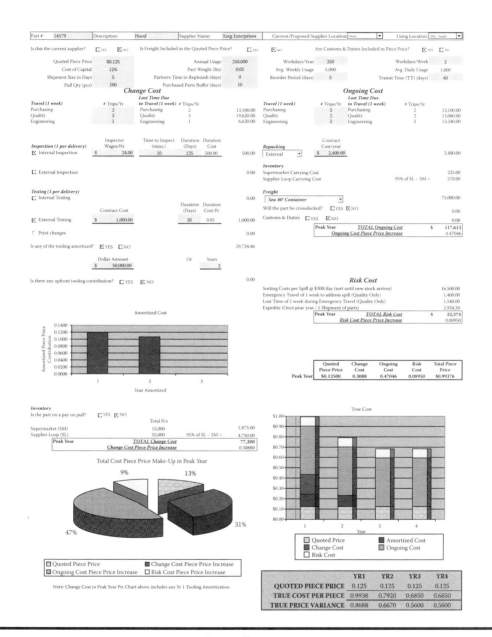

Figure 11.12 Part # 14579 Proposed Supplier.

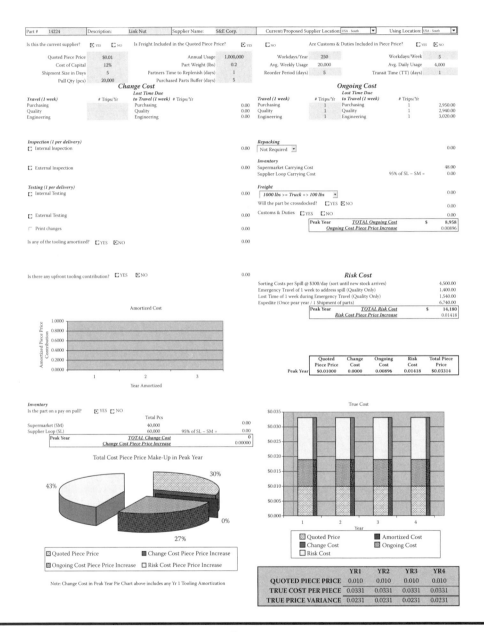

Figure 11.13   Part # 14224 Current Supplier.

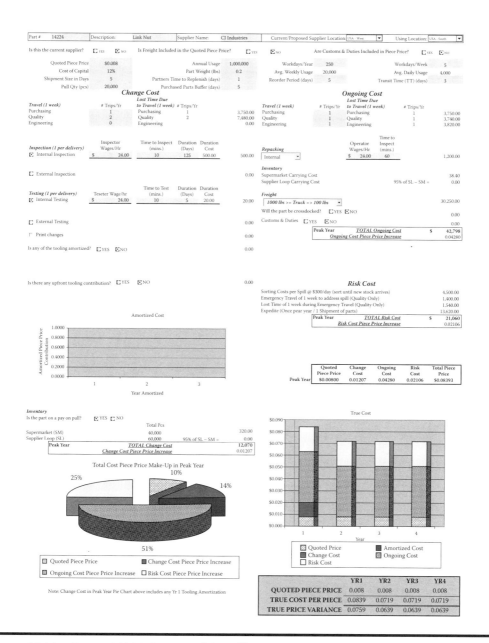

Figure 11.14   Part # 14224 Proposed Supplier.

supplier over the current supplier. If this supplier were judged on piece price alone, they would not even be in the competition. When they are looked at on a level playing field based on true cost, it is quickly revealed that they are competitive, regardless of what was initially thought (Figures 11.15 and 11.16).

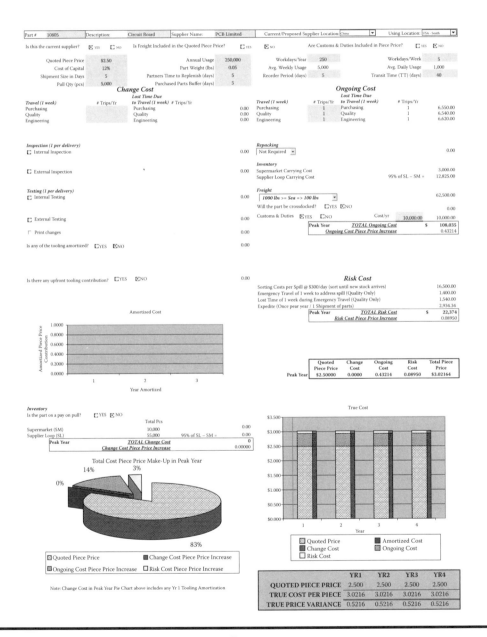

Figure 11.15 Part # 10805 Current Supplier.

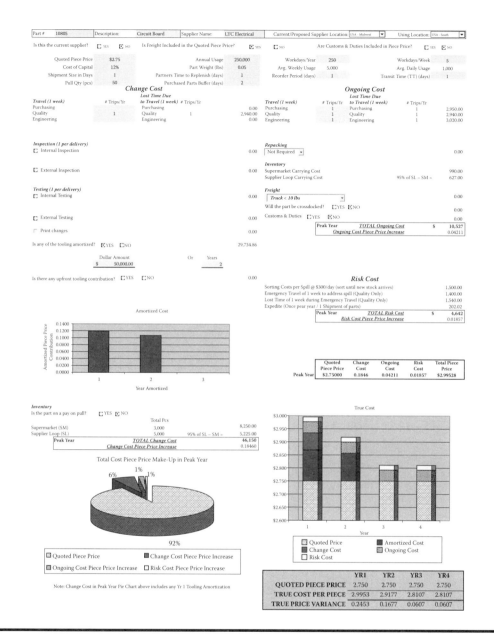

Figure 11.16   10805 Proposed Supplier.

Conclusion

Through our hypothetical examples, we've shown you how to create and use a model to evaluate the true cost of a part—not just the piece price—to evaluate suppliers and determine the cost viability of an organization.

We must remind you that no decision should be based on cost alone. The current relationship, quality level, delivery performance, and other factors should all play a key role in your examination of supplier selection and partner development. But you can't ignore what the part is actually costing you. By using the model methodology described in this chapter, you can determine your own true costs, thereby making more informed supplier development decisions.

INTERACTIONS BETWEEN LEAN CUSTOMERS AND PARTNERS

IV

Chapter 12

Understanding the Physical Connection between Partner and Customer

Introduction

In this chapter, we'll outline the physical connection, or informational link, between the partner and the customer, in the form of pull signals. This chapter explains the mathematical formula for determining the number of pull signals that will be needed to effectively support your production system.

You need to be able to understand and use the formula to correctly size the pull loop, or information loop, between your facility and your supply partner. Since this will be the way parts are continually ordered, it's critical that your calculations be correct.

Pull Signals: The Informational Link

Once you've chosen the supplier that you want to develop into a partner, you need to consider how you will communicate with that partner on a regular basis. Specifically, you need an information transfer letting the partner know that you have used a component and that you need another one. The informational link that we use is called a pull signal.

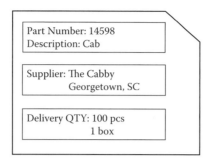

Figure 12.1   Kanban card.

A pull signal can take various forms, but we recommend the kanban* card; it seems to be the most common way to communicate with suppliers, and we have had a lot of success using the kanban card mentality. When parts are received into the facility, each box, pallet of material, or standard quantity of material should correspond to the kanban card that was used to request that part. Figure 12.1 is an illustration of a kanban card.

In essence, the kanban card represents an order for a specific component. The card then stays with the box of components as it enters the purchased parts supermarket, and is removed when the material is collected and moved out of the supermarket to the production area. The card is then given to the person responsible for reordering the parts. That person can either reorder the parts right away or can hold the cards until he or she gets the necessary number, or a minimum reorder quantity, of cards to reorder the components. However, it's our hope that any supplier that you partner with will not require a minimum reorder quantity of anything larger than one standard pack.

The key to this simple reordering system is the number of pull signals in the loop. If you have too few pull signals in the loop, you run the danger of running out of parts, because you haven't given your supplier adequate time to replenish them. If you have too many cards in the loop, then you will likely carry more inventory than you actually need, because the supplier will be delivering more product than is required to support your production operations.

---

* A kanban card is a card that holds information about a standard pack of parts—part number, quantity, supermarket location, supplier, etc.

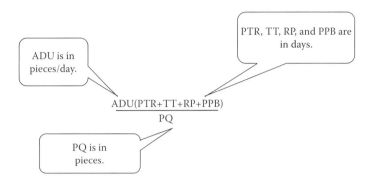

Figure 12.2 Formula to size supplier pull signal loop.

How to Size the Number of Pull Signals between Partner and Customer

The formula that we use to calculate the number of pull signals in the loop between the partner and the customer takes a number of variables into account; in this section, we will outline those variables and explain how to calculate the number of pull signals you need to connect your organization with your partner.

The formula is average daily usage (ADU) times the sum of the partner's time to replenish the parts (PTR), transit time (TT), reorder period (RP), and purchased parts buffer (PPB), divided by the pull quantity (PQ). In its mathematical form it is as shown in Figure 12.2.

Note that if you have a situation in which your reorder period does not match the frequency at which you receive material, you'll need to alter the formula to account for that difference.

Average Daily Usage (ADU)

Average daily usage (ADU) is the average daily demand for a component. There are a number of things to keep in mind when you're using this calculation. Notably, if you are calculating the daily usage on a component that you run only once per month, ADU will likely not work for you, because you're running a batch of product when you use this component, rather than using the component daily. In these cases, your daily demand will appear to be a low level even though it may be accurate because when you run the product, you actually run a higher quantity. Our formula won't work for these parts; it's designed for parts that you use often. If you run batches of material, you should not order them in a manner designed for product run on a daily basis; these parts need to be ordered on an as-needed basis.

You'll also need to deal differently with components that have a low usage quantity. Low-usage parts are often best ordered on an as-needed basis. Anything that is not run in a high enough quantity to utilize the daily demand should be handled differently and ordered on an as-needed basis.

Partner's Time to Replenish (PTR)

Partner's time to replenish is the time from when the order is received until the day before the order ships. This time could include the production time, and any other wait time between when the product is complete and the shipping day.

Calculate the PTR from experience, not promises. Although you've chosen this supplier to be your partner, you still need to calculate your pull signal size based upon realistic data. If the PTR is wrong, then the rest of the formula will also be incorrect. PTR is calculated in business days.

Transit Time (TT)

Transit time is the time that it takes for the components to be shipped from your partner to your purchased parts supermarket. This includes any time added for parts sitting on your receiving dock, incoming inspection (which we hope to avoid), as well as the actual transport time (by truck, boat, plane, rail, etc.). Be sure to include any waiting time that the material experiences between the partner and customer.

Reorder Period (RP)

The reorder period is the time between orders. For example, if you reorder product from the partner every Monday, the reorder period would be 5, assuming that your facility operates on a five-day workweek. If you work a seven-day workweek, your reorder period would be 7.

In a perfect world, our partners would accept orders every day, leading to fewer pull signals in the system, making the reorder period 1. The reorder period is calculated in business days.

Purchased Parts Buffer (PPB)

Our purchased parts buffer (PPB) is the same as it is for the planned maximum inventory (see Chapter 6), except in this case it is represented in business days. Again, a purchased parts buffer is used as insurance against potential mishaps (weather, quality, etc.) that can potentially cause your facility to run out of product.

Pull Quantity (PQ)

The pull quantity (PQ) is the quantity (in pieces) in which the parts are ordered and received as defined on the supplier kanban card for the part. In most cases, the pull quantity is equal to the standard pack (SP), typically a one-box quantity. When dealing with internal material movement, the standard pack is almost always determined by box or small container because those parts are delivered directly to associates on the production floor.

For pull signal sizes between the partner and supplier, it may be appropriate to determine the pull quantity by the case, pallet, or skid of material. If you use a high quantity of a part, or if your partner is a long distance from your facility, you may choose to use a multiple of the standard pack size, such as a pallet versus the standard pack of a box.

Remember, you can order and receive a different pull quantity from your partner than you use in your internal material delivery system. For example, you may order parts by the pallet from your supply partner, but you consume them based upon the box inside your facility (Figure 12.3).

Examples of Loop Size Calculations

Part Number 14598

Let's calculate the loop size for part number 14598. The calculation shows that there will be thirty-five pull signals in the loop between the partner and the customer, or a constant flow of thirty-five pull signals between the partner and the supplier. This calculation is pretty straightforward, with a PTR of 1, TT of 1, RP of 1, and PPB of a half day. Think of the formula this way: there is one day being produced at the partner, one day in transit, one day at the customer, plus a half day of buffer. That is how you can account for the 3.5 days of inventory (Figure 12.4).

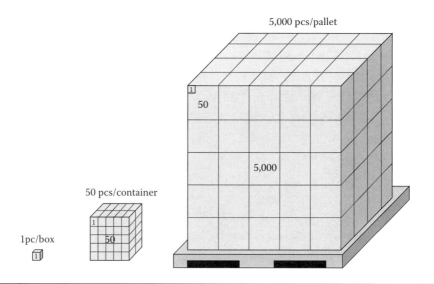

Figure 12.3   Different types of consumption.

Part Number 14598

$$\frac{1,000(1+1+1+0.5)}{100}$$

35 Pull Signals

Figure 12.4   Loop Size Calculation for Part Number 14598.

Part Number 14579

For part number 14579, we need to have 235 pull signals in the loop, or in constant movement, between the partner and the customer. Why the larger number of pull signals in this loop? It takes the supplier fourteen days to process, produce, and prepare the ordered product shipment, and we're only ordering product one time per week (see Figure 12.5).

Part Number 14556

The calculation for part number 14556 could have a very large number of pull signals in the system. If we pulled by the box (SP), we'll see 3,700 pull signals in the loop between the supplier and the customer. If the product is

Part Number 14579

$$\frac{1,000(14+2+5+2.5)}{100}$$

235 Pull Signals

Figure 12.5   Loop Size Calculation for Part Number 14579.

pulled and delivered by the pallet, with one hundred boxes per pallet, the number goes down to thirty-seven pull signals. Why are there so many pull signals in this particular loop? Most likely, this is the result of the distance between the supplier and the customer and their poor response time to order. It takes them a maximum seventy-five days before they can ship product once they receive a signal, and the total transit time on water, rail, truck, and internal inspection takes forty-five days (Figure 12.6). It is because of this situation that the SP and the PQ differ in the Plan for Every Part (PFEP).

Part Number: 14556

$$\frac{1,000(75+45+60+5)}{50}$$

3,700 Pull Signals

Part Number: 14556

$$\frac{1,000(75+45+60+5)}{5,000}$$

37 Pull Signals if by Pallet (100 boxes per)

Figure 12.6   Loop Size Calculation for Part Number 14556.

Part Number: 14224

$$\frac{4,000(1+1+5+5)}{20,000}$$

3 (2.4) Pull Signals (Have to round up)

Figure 12.7   Loop Size Calculation for Part Number 14224.

Part Number 14224

Part number 14224 has the smallest number of pull signals in the group, with only three in the loop, given a large standard pack, pull quantity, the short replenishment time (1 day) and transit time from the partner. An interesting note on this part number is that the calculation indicates that there should be 2.4 pull signals in the loop; however, you can't order part of a pull signal because a pull signal represents one complete pull quantity of parts. Pull signal calculations should always be rounded up to ensure that you don't have a shortage of parts for the production facility (Figure 12.7).

Part Number 14997

This part number has 120 pull signals in the loop, since it takes five days for the supplier to replenish product, and the part is ordered only once a week (Figure 12.8).

Part Number: 14997

$$\frac{1,000(5+1+5+1)}{100}$$

120 Pull Signals

Figure 12.8   Loop Size Calculation for Part Number 14997.

Part Number 14448

This part number could also have a large number of pull signals, probably because of the distance between the supplier and the customer. If you pulled by boxes (SP), the number of pull signals is thirteen thousand, but if the calculation is made by pallet, the pull loop size is sixty-five. With a 40-day replenishment time, a 30-day transit time, and a 120-day reorder period, the pull loop size, again, is large. It is because of this situation that the SP and the PQ differ in the PFEP (Figure 12.9).

Part Number 10805

The calculation for part number 10805 indicates a very large number of pull signals in the system. Pulling by the box (SP), there are 1,100 pull signals in the loop between the supplier and the customer. If the product is pulled by the pallet and delivered by the pallet, with one hundred boxes per pallet, the number of pull signals goes down to eleven. Again, the SP and the PQ differ in the PFEP due to this issue (Figure 12.10).

Part Number: 14448

$$\frac{1,000(40+30+120+5)}{15}$$

13,000 Pull Signals

Part Number: 14448

$$\frac{1,000(40+30+120+5)}{3,000}$$

65 Pull Signals if by Pallet (200 boxes per)

Figure 12.9 Loop Size Calculation for Part Number 14448.

Part Number: 10805

$$\frac{1,000(5+40+5+5)}{50}$$

1,100 Pull Signals

Part Number: 10805

$$\frac{1,000(5+40+5+5)}{5,000}$$

11 Pull Signals if by Pallet (100 boxes per)

Figure 12.10   Loop Size Calculation for Part Number 10805.

Reasons to Drive Down Pull Signal Loop Size

Pull signals represent material in your supply chain; the larger the number of pull signals in your pull loop, the more material is in your supply chain.

Material costs are a large portion of the cost of goods sold (COGS). When you begin implementation of your Lean supplier development initiatives, you need to be aware of the high cost of material and take steps to improve these efficiencies. You want your supply base to run at the minimal material levels sustainable for your company.

Conclusion

Pull signals are a simple and effective way to communicate with your partners. By being aware of the variables that impact pull signals, it's hopeful that you'll not run out of product or, conversely, find yourself with excessive inventory on hand. In the next chapter, we'll talk about what happens once your pull signals are in place and you're receiving incoming material from your supplier partner.

Chapter 13

Receiving Product

Introduction

In this chapter, we'll cover how to handle incoming material from your supply partners. We will also cover how to handle the actual pull signals discussed in the previous chapter. Many facilities batch receive incoming material, but there's a better way.

We can't stress this enough: don't leave any loose ends in your system. You don't want to go through all of the work of developing partners just to leave the rest of your system to chance. In this chapter, we'll explain how to get the parts from the truck to the purchased parts market more efficiently.

Receiving Windows

What do we mean when we say that many facilities batch receive incoming material? We mean that in the mornings, much of the product ordered is received into the system on a first-come, first-served basis. This means that the afternoon is slower, and the off shifts (second and third) do little receiving, if any (Figure 13.1).

Most facilities allow suppliers to ship product as the suppliers choose. Many facilities do not control incoming material in a way that levels the workload of the receiving department. You want to level the incoming material workload because it provides us with a more reliable and efficient way

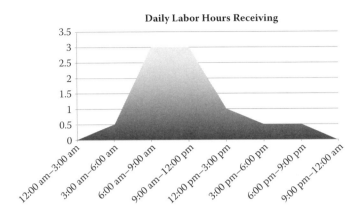

Figure 13.1 Daily labor hours receiving.

to get the parts from the receiving dock to the purchased parts market. Since the parts aren't ready for production until they're in the purchased parts supermarket, we need to get the product from the truck to the purchased parts supermarket as efficiently as possible.

To level the incoming material workload, we use receiving windows. A receiving window is a specific time of the day and week assigned to a supply partner; the supply partner is only allowed to deliver product during that time span. Receiving windows are typically an hour; this means that there is a span of one hour on a particular day that the partner is allowed to deliver the product. Let's take a look at what receiving windows may look like for suppliers on the Plan for Every Part (PFEP) that we have been using throughout this book (Figure 13.2).

By leveling workloads and increasing efficiency in the receiving department, receiving windows should lead to fewer errors and less waiting time between the receiving dock and the purchased parts market. Receiving windows also provide necessary data for better sizing the purchased parts supermarket. When a partner can be relied on to deliver product every Wednesday at 9:00 a.m., for example, a facility can plan its inventory levels accordingly, but if a supplier delivers its parts every Wednesday at 9:00 a.m., plus or minus two days, extra inventory must be carried in the purchased parts supermarket to cover the discrepancy.

Receiving windows allow for a more efficient and productive Lean enterprise supply chain. When material flow is leveled, the planning department can plan for stability.

	Monday	*Tuesday*	*Wednesday*	*Thursday*	*Friday*
7:00-8:00am					
8:00-9:00am		PCB Limited	J&C Inc		
9:00-10:00am	S&E Corp				
10:00-11:00am				Molding Ideas	
11:00-12:00pm	The Cabby	The Cabby	The Cabby	The Cabby	The Cabby
1:00-2:00pm		Comfy Beds			
2:00-3:00pm				Frames R Us	
3:00-4:00pm					

Figure 13.2   Receiving windows.

Receiving Boards

Next, let's talk about how to physically manage pull signals. As you begin to learn this system, you should start with physical kanban cards. Once you feel comfortable with the concepts and the running of the partner–customer relations, you may choose to move to electronic kanbans for external material movement. In our experience, physical cards are still most effective for handling internal material movement and when you first begin developing suppliers.

When using physical cards, you need to be able to identify which cards have been used to order parts. We like to use a receiving board, which holds the kanban cards after they have been used to order components (Figures 13.3 and 13.4).

Once the card has been used to order components, the card is placed on the receiving board to indicate that the material is incoming. When the corresponding material is received, the kanban card is taken from the receiving board and placed on the parts, after which both the card and parts are placed in their dedicated location in the purchased parts supermarket. When the parts and the kanban card are in the purchased parts supermarket, the

Receiving Board
(Mon the 2nd at 7 am)

	MON	TUE	WED	THU	FRI
Week 19	2 — PRT#1450R PRT#14224 20,000 pcs S&E Corp	3 — PRT#10805 PRT#14448 120,000 pcs Comfy Beds	4 — PRT#14579 100 pcs I&C Inc.	5 — PRT#14997 100 pcs Molding Ideas	6
Week 20	9 — PRT#14224 20,000 pcs S&E Corp	10 — PRT#10805 5,000 pcs PCB Limited	11	12 — PRT#14556 60,000 pcs Frames RUs	13
Week 21	16 — PRT#14224 20,000 pcs S&E Corp	17 — PRT#10805 5,000 PCB Limited	18	19	20
Week 22	23 — HOLIDAY	24 — PRT#10805 5,000 pcs PCB Limited	25	26	27
Week 23	30	31 — PRT#10805 5,000 pcs PCB Limited	1	2	3
Week 24	6	7 — PRT#10805 5,000 pcs PCB Limited	8	9	10

= Current Day   = Current Week

Figure 13.3 Receiving board.

Receiving Board
3 Weeks Later
(Tue the 24th at 7 am)

	MON	TUE	WED	THU	FRI
Week 25	13 PRT# 14224 20,000 pcs S&E Corp	14 PRT# 10805 5,000 pcs PCB Limited	15	16	17
Week 26	20	21 PRT# 10805 5,000 pcs PCB Limited	22	23	24
Week 27	27	28 PRT# 10805 5,000 pcs PCB Limited	29	30	31
Week 22	23 HOLIDAY	24 PRT# 14598 / PRT# 10805 100 pcs PCB Limited	25 PRT# 14579 100 pcs J&C Inc.	26 PRT#14997 100 pcs Molding Ideas	27
Week 23	30 PRT# 14224 20,000 pcs S&E Corp	31 PRT# 10805 5,000 pcs PCB Limited	1	2	3
Week 24	6 PRT# 14224 20,000 pcs S&E Corp	7 PRT# 10805 5,000 pcs PCB Limited	8	9	10

= Current Week

= Current Day

Figure 13.4 Receiving board.

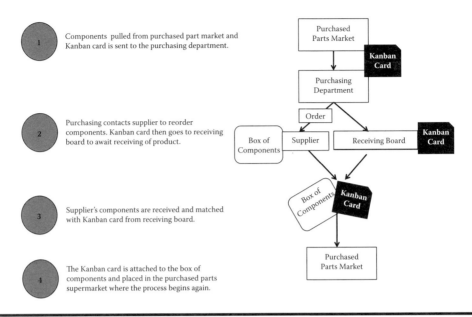

1 Components pulled from purchased part market and Kanban card is sent to the purchasing department.

2 Purchasing contacts supplier to reorder components. Kanban card then goes to receiving board to await receiving of product.

3 Supplier's components are received and matched with Kanban card from receiving board.

4 The Kanban card is attached to the box of components and placed in the purchased parts supermarket where the process begins again.

Figure 13.5   Flow of information and material between partner and customer.

system can begin again. An added benefit of using the receiving board is that if there is a kanban card on the receiving board after the date that the parts were to be delivered, it serves as an indicator that a part did not arrive on time and that action needs to be taken. Figure 13.5 illustrates this flow of information and material.

Other Methods of Interacting with Suppliers

Electronic systems present an excellent way to interact with supply partners, but if you can't do something manually, an electronic system most likely can't do it for you.

It's best to start small when beginning to use this pull signal system; learning how the system works is the most important thing in the beginning phases of implementation. This way, you can learn on a small scale how to size and handle the pull signals and the best way to use this information to interact with your partners. By starting small, with only one supply partner and physical kanban cards, you can learn a great deal without impacting a great deal of people and organizations. If you try to implement too large and too fast, there is a risk of shutting down operations or alienating future partners as a result of a learning curve that could have happened on a small scale.

Once you learn all of the ins and outs of the system and how it works best for your organization and your partners, you can begin to look into forms of technology that can enhance your system. In most cases, you shouldn't build your systems around technology. Lean enterprise systems are more efficient when we first design them to flow effectively and then implement technology that enhances that flow, rather than procuring the most up-to-date technology first and hoping it makes material flow. In short, design your systems to flow, and then find technologies that enhance your flow, always taking the necessary steps to continually improve your system.

Conclusion

Receiving windows are an effective tool for leveling the load of incoming material and providing an environment for improved efficiencies for the receiving department. The receiving board is a good tool to learn how to handle your pull signals and interact with your partner.

Finally, once you understand the system of pull signals and partner interaction in great detail, technology can be an excellent way to enhance the flow of value (material) in your Lean enterprise supply chain. Design your system for flow first, and then add technology to enhance the flow.

Once you've implemented your pull system and leveled your incoming material loads, you can start refining your packaging. We'll go into component packaging in Chapter 14.

Chapter 14

Packaging

Introduction

When you're working with your suppliers to obtain the packaging that is most efficient for your system, you need to focus on three things: the quantity of components in the package, cardboard containers versus returnable containers, and how many standard size containers you should have in your facility. In this chapter, we'll discuss all three of these issues.

Standard Pack Quantity

It is imperative that you receive the same quantity per box *every time* that you receive product from the supplier. Standard pack quantities mean that the part always comes in the same quantity per pack from the supplier. For example, if we look at our Plan for Every Part (PFEP), we see that part number 14598 has a standard box quantity of one hundred pieces. This means that every time a box of part number 14598 arrives from the supplier, there should be one hundred pieces in the box.

It's important for the pack quantities to be standardized because almost all of the calculations for internal material movement are based upon standard quantities. Without standard quantities, planning for material movement becomes very difficult; conversely, ensuring that there are standard quantities in each container allows you to plan for effective material

movement in your facilities, which in turn will likely lead to a more efficient facility.

So now that we know that production facilities cannot handle non-stan-
dard-pack quantities, or at least can't handle them well, the question then
becomes: What should the standard quantity be? The standard box quantity
should be a quantity that evenly goes into the finished goods pack quantity.
For example, continuing with part number 14598, the finished goods pack-
out quantity is fifty pieces. This means that when the facility runs this part,
they likely run fifty of them, because the customer buys the product in that
quantity. But for a finished goods pack quantity of fifty, the standard pack
quantity of one hundred parts is too high.

Why is the box quantity too high? It limits the flexibility of the facility. Whenever the facility wants to run this part, it has to run at least two
finished goods packs to use one box of this part number. In a flexible
Lean enterprise environment, the goal is to make what the customer wants,
when the customer wants it. If the customer wants one finished goods
pack of fifty, then that's what you should produce. If the facility runs just
one finished goods pack with the current standard package quantity, it
then either has to transport the partially full containers of components
back to its purchased parts market or store the remaining parts at the point
of use (POU). This can cause inefficiencies, including the *waste* of either
taking the purchased components away from the production area, back to
the purchased parts market, or storing more than two hours of material at
the POU.

Some facilities choose not to take the partially filled containers back to
the supermarket, and instead keep them in the production area. This causes
a flow problem. What happens when the components are needed again?
There has to be some mechanism in place to make sure that those parts are
pulled first so that first in, first out (FIFO) remains intact. So now, in addition
to the system currently used to deliver product to the production areas, we
need to develop *another* system to ensure that we use the partial container
first. In short, partial containers cause a lot of unneeded stress on the production system.

If the standard box quantity is 2, 5, 10, 25, or 50, you won't have to take
partially filled containers back to the supermarket where they are stored.
Now, the facility has the flexibility to make any number of finished goods
pack-out quantities that they choose because these box quantities easily go
into the finished goods pack-out quantity.

So why is this even an issue? The box quantities that you receive are possibly a result of the part being purchased at a cheaper price in that specific box quantity. However, if you were to take a look at the total cost of dealing with this material, you may find that it actually costs you *more* to allow the supplier to dictate your box quantities, because of the inefficiencies that it causes in your internal material movement system.

Box quantities are simple to explain, but can be difficult to attack. If you begin to attack the box quantities before you develop your suppliers, you may find the cost of changing box quantities prohibitive. But if you wait until you're developing your suppliers into partners, you may find them much more amenable to your requests—as long as you don't make them too often!

A key point in this discussion is the high level of quality needed to make all of this happen. If a supplier's product is of poor quality, it really does not matter what the box quantity is because you cannot plan according to standard numbers. Let's revisit our previous discussion of box quantity. If there is fallout because of quality and your box quantity is fifty, then you will have to bring out a whole box to cover the difference, which of course causes major flow and leveling problems with purchased components within the system. If you currently have quality problems in your system, you are likely experiencing costly production problems already. In a Lean production system, they're easier to identify because you can immediately see the impact. This system is set up to run on perfect quality from suppliers, so quality problems immediately impact the system, letting management know that action needs to be taken. So, by developing suppliers into high-quality partners, this system allows your production system to be more efficient. Poor quality always disrupts the flow of product, and when the flow of product is disrupted, it costs the facility efficiencies—and efficiencies equal money.

Cardboard Boxes or Plastic Returnable Containers

You might think that this is an easy call, but deciding whether to use cardboard boxes or plastic returnable containers requires some thought. Cardboard containers do lead to extra trash in the facility. However, there is no need to worry about returning the cardboard containers back to the supplier.

One of the major determinants of whether or not to utilize returnable containers is the distance of the supplier from your facility. When dealing with a supplier from another continent, it is very difficult to use returnable containers, as the cost of transport will likely be very high. However, when a supplier is in close proximity to your facility, returnable containers can make more sense.

When you buy returnable containers, you have a one-time material cost, the cost of the containers. When you use cardboard boxes, you have to pay for the box every time that you buy the component. This cost can be substantial if the component is used often.

Both returnable containers and cardboard have after-use cost. The after-use cost of returnable containers is the cost of transporting the containers back to the supplier and maintaining them. The after-use cost of cardboard is the cost of disposal or recycling. This cost can be higher than you realize when you take into account the labor, storage, and actual disposal costs together.

Another variable to think about when deciding on cardboard versus returnable containers is the true cost model. You may be able to tweak your total cost model to help with the decision. For example, you have to open a cardboard box and dispose of a cardboard box. How much does that cost each time it has to be done? How much does each box cost? How much does a returnable container cost? You may not have to open them or dispose of them, but you do have to return them to your supplier, keep them clean, and replace them as needed. Do the math and determine which is better for your facility's Lean enterprise system.

Five Standard Sizes

One of the big benefits of returnable containers is that you can standardize the sizes throughout the facility, which can streamline the internal logistics of the facility. For example, let's say that your facility has made a decision to use five standard sizes of containers. These five sizes are classified as very small, small, medium, large, and very large.

Now that you know that any purchased component from your suppliers will come in one of these five standard size containers, you can plan accordingly. Your internal material movement system will likely have less stress dealing with five standard size containers than it would dealing with all different sizes of containers, because the conveyance system (tugger*) can be designed to only move all five sizes of containers.

Furthermore, designing the work area also becomes easier for the engineers in the facility. They can examine the production area and determine which of the five standard sizes of containers is best for the value-added operator (production associate) to perform the value-added work and notify purchasing as to what size the container should be. Then the engineers can proceed to design a workspace that provides value to the customer and eliminates (or at least minimizes) waste.

In this case, both the box size and quantity are determined based on the efficiency of the system and not the piece price cost of the component. This is likely the more appropriate way to make decisions on container size and quantity, because it is based on the value-added operator and efficient production system, and not solely on a piece price cost that is not representative of the total cost to the Lean enterprise system.

Conclusion

Although each facility is different, you'll need to address three issues when working with suppliers to obtain packaging that is most efficient for the system: the quantity of product in the package, whether to use cardboard or returnable containers, and how many standard size containers to use.

Our goal in this chapter was to provide you with a different way to think about containerization in your facility in hopes that the decisions on containerization will go from the supplier's best interest to the best interest of your Lean enterprise system as a whole.

In Chapter 15, we'll discuss how to actually choose your first supplier to develop into a partner.

---

* A tugger is a vehicle that can pull a large amount of product and deliver to multiple production areas on a route. This route is designed much like a bus route with multiple stops on a timed schedule.

DEVELOP A SUPPLIER INTO A PARTNER

Chapter 15

The Partner Development Team

Introduction

Now, armed with enough information to choose a supplier to become a partner, your next task is to actually choose that first supplier. After you choose your first partner supplier, your next step is to determine how to develop that supplier into a partner.

This chapter will lead you through both a thought process of how to choose your first supplier for a long-term partnership and a model for developing and improving suppliers into partners. This model is designed as a teaching model, in hopes that at the end of the process, partners are able to continually improve on their own without outside support.

Choosing Your First Supplier to Develop into a Partner

In Chapter 4, we listed ten attributes to consider when choosing a supplier to develop into a partner. Taking these attributes into consideration, it's now time to choose your first supplier to develop. Success is the key when developing your first supplier into a long-term partnership. It is very important that the first supplier you choose to develop is a big success, because the organization will be watching this new initiative and will likely begin to form opinions early on in the process. We want to make sure that everyone has a positive impression on the supplier-partner program. To help ensure success, we have developed some important variables to consider when choosing the first supplier to develop: distance, quality, on-time delivery, and desire.

You need to consider distance when choosing the first supplier to develop into a partner because of the number of times that your partner development team, which we'll discuss in the following pages, will travel to the supplier. When you're developing your first supplier into a partner, you'll likely conduct more visits, in a shorter amount of time, than you will when your partner development team has more experience. Consequently, it's safer in the beginning to choose a supplier that is a close distance to your facility. It may even be best to choose a supplier within a short driving distance, if possible, because that way your partner development team can simply jump in the car and get to the supplier quickly if need be.

Quality is your second important variable; in the beginning, you want your partner development team to focus on developing the Lean connections between your organization and the supplier. Poor quality disrupts the flow of value and will draw a lot of negative attention to everyone involved. During future development projects, you may find that you need to focus on fixing some of the quality problems of the supplier. At that point, you may want to send in some of your quality practitioners to assist in fixing the problems. However, the first supplier that you choose should have very limited, if any, quality problems. It is important to remember to start your implementation efforts on a small scale to increase the likelihood of success. The first supplier is the most important because everyone is learning together to create long-term partnerships in the supply chain. Future efforts will depend on the knowledge that is gained by the partner development team as well as the rest of the organization in the early implementation efforts.

On-time delivery is your third variable to consider when choosing the first supplier to develop. Your first supplier should have a history of delivering product on time. Delivering product on time is a basic function of a supplier and is one that should not be an issue when choosing the first supplier to develop. Again, you want your focus to be on the Lean connections between the supplier and your facility during the first partnership, not on other items that should be assumed to be acceptable, such as quality and on-time delivery.

Desire is the last variable that we talk about when choosing the first supplier to develop into a partner. You need to choose a supplier that has a desire for a long-term relationship, and whose leadership is committed to continuous improvement. Developing suppliers into partners is not only for your benefit, but also for your supplier's benefit; you're only as healthy as your supply base, so it is important for your suppliers to be successful as well.

Again, these variables apply specifically to the first supplier you choose to develop. Why do we put so much emphasis on your first supplier? If your first supplier development initiative goes well, you will likely have more support within your organization as you begin to develop other suppliers into partners. On the opposite side of the spectrum, if you fail in your first attempt to develop a supplier into a partner, you'll probably have a difficult time gaining support to develop other suppliers in the future.

Also, remember that you'll have a learning curve when you develop your first supplier. As much as possible, you need to set yourself up for success before you begin, so choosing the right supplier to begin with is vital. Make sure that everyone understands that this is a learning experience and that future supplier development will likely go more smoothly; further, you can choose more difficult suppliers to work with in the future if necessary.

Forming a Partner Development Team

The first step after choosing a supplier to develop into a partner is to designate a team of Lean practitioners within your facility to tackle partner development. Again, you should only begin to develop suppliers *after* you have had a great deal of success in implementing your own Lean production system. The reason is that if you have had a great deal of success implementing your own Lean production system, you have likely developed some very capable Lean practitioners in your facility through your years of implementation—and you'll need those practitioners now.

Your partner development team is different than the other key players outlined earlier in this book. The partner development team is a team of Lean practitioners that are capable of assisting an organization in a transition from their current production methods to a Lean production system. There is a difference between Lean book knowledge and Lean implementation knowledge: implementation knowledge means that an individual has both the Lean book knowledge *and* the implementation experience to change from a traditional production system to a Lean enterprise system. This knowledge is another reason that implementing Lean in your own facility first is so valuable. Your partner development team members will have assisted your facility or facilities in changing from your old system of production to your new system, based on Lean production principles.

Through your Lean implementation to date you have likely attacked your production areas, material flow, quality, maintenance, scheduling, and business processes. When forming your partner development team, it is a good idea to recruit a staff member from each of these areas. So, a solid partner development team may include the following:

- A representative from production
- A representative from material flow
- A representative from quality
- A representative from maintenance
- A representative from scheduling
- A value stream specialist—the partner development team leader

You'll need to assign one person as the leader of this team. Typically, the person most prepared to lead the partner development team has extensive experience in using the value stream methodology to implementation (we'll talk more about this in Chapter 16). You need one individual in the leadership role to make decisions about where to focus your improvement efforts. The value stream methodology will guide the improvement efforts in suppliers' facilities, and it is important that you have someone who understands the methodology, who can choose where to focus efforts, and who can decide which members of the team need to play a specific role in the development and implementation of those efforts.

The Teaching Mentality of the Partner Development Team

When deciding how the partner development team will interact with the chosen supplier, it is important to remember that the end goal is success for both parties involved. Therefore, it is important to teach your supplier how to develop and continually improve their Lean enterprise system. Your partner development team won't implement the Lean enterprise system for the supplier, but will teach the supplier how to implement the system.

To ensure that this happens, you need to choose and follow a methodology of implementation. The supplier teaching method that we adhere to is based on short monthly visits that include assignments for the next visit. For example, your first visit to your chosen supplier might last two days. During these two days, you'll give your supplier an overview of the Lean enterprise system, you'll choose a product family that impacts both the supplier and the customer, and you'll draw up a current state and start a future state map. Finally, you'll give the supplier assignments to be completed by the next month's visit.

After the first visit, it will be up to your partner development team to decide whether the visits are to be held biweekly or monthly. Many suppliers go through *phases* of implementation. During the first, or beginning, phase, two- to three-day biweekly visits may be appropriate to effectively launch the implementation. This phase may last from three to twelve months. In the second phase, when the supplier begins to see the benefits of Lean enterprise and understands the process, the need for biweekly visits will likely fall to two- to three-day monthly visits. This phase can last from one to four years. The third phase will only require one day per month, when the supplier uses the partner development team as a resource to assist them with problems that they run into. During the fourth and final phase of implementation, the supplier will call the partner development team for specific issues; visits from the team are scheduled accordingly on an as-needed basis. The goal at this point is for the supplier to have gained enough knowledge to continue Lean enterprise implementation on their own.

You'll need to follow specific agendas to run the visits effectively and efficiently. Figures 15.1 and 15.2 show examples of the first two days' agendas.

Agendas need to be developed before each visit. On the first and second days, it is the partner development team's responsibility to create the agenda. After the second day, the supplier should develop the agenda with input from the partner development team leader. Why are agendas so important? These visits need to be about identifying and addressing items in the value stream that eliminate waste and improve the production lead time, and you don't want to spend half the day trying to determine where to work. Although you may not follow the agenda to the letter, you won't waste time identifying what needs to be addressed.

Who Gets the Savings?

A major issue to be addressed concerns the money that will be saved through the implementation of Lean enterprise principles within suppliers' value streams. You need to tread very carefully here. If you and your partner

Day 1

7:00–8:00   Arrive, meet plant management and discuss the day
8:00–9:00   Plant Assessment walk

*   Partner Development Team to walk facility with key leadership and assess current state and opportunities asking many questions on the walk. The walk always begins at shipping (Closest to Customer). Focus on the three manufacturing flows.

9:00–9:30   Review Walk with Key Management
9:30–12:00   Lean 101

*   Including Breakout session and report back. Break into 7 groups. Assign each group a waste to find. The Session is focused on finding waste on the production floor.
*   Feel free to state what you saw on the assessment walk.

12:00–1:00   Lunch
1:00–4:00   Value Stream Mapping

*   Check to see the current situation as it pertains to Value Stream mapping. The goal for the rest of this day is to give the participants enough information to go to the floor and draw the Current VSM and have them complete the Current VSM. Current VSM information and material flow is necessary to have completed at the end of Day 1.

Figure 15.1   Sample agenda.

development team go into a facility and make it about getting money back instead of developing a long-term partnership, there could be disastrous results.

If you play a major role in the development of suppliers and the implementation of their Lean enterprise systems, then you are certainly entitled to share in the savings; in our experience, the most that you should ask for and receive is 50% of the savings. There must be some incentive for the suppliers to utilize your partner development team and embrace Lean enterprise, but to emphasize that this is a true partnership, 50% of the savings is the most that you should take.

Day 2

7:00–8:00   Discuss the collection of data for the Current VSM.

8:00–12:00 In-depth discussion of Future State Value Stream Mapping

12:00–1:00 Lunch

1:00–3:00   Develop the Future State Map

3:00–4:00   Wrap up and Homework assignments
- What needs to be completed before the next visit to help achieve the future state?
- Who is responsible for the task?
- Who is going to develop the next visit's agenda?

*** Need to have a a good draft FUTURE STATE AND AN ITEMIZED LIST OF TO DO ITEMS WITH NAMES AND DATES OF THOSE RESPONSIBLE.

***NEED TO HAVE FIRM UNDERSTANDING OF WHO IS RESPONSIBLE FOR NEXT VISIT AGENDA. That agenda should include checking on ALL of the previous visit's homework assignments.

***Be sure to tell whoever is in charge of the next agenda that you need an hour at the beginning to discuss a Glass Wall procedure that will be used beginning with the second visit.

Figure 15.2   Sample agenda.

However, determining the amount of savings will not be easy if you and the supplier do not identify an effective measurement system before you start the process. This is why the glass wall* is utilized, so that the beginning numbers are known to everyone from the start. There must be ample trust between the supplier and you, the customer, since typically suppliers are very reluctant to let customers look at the books. This whole thought process may be very different than you are accustomed to in supplier-customer relations, but it is a must to form true partnerships that are beneficial for the entire supply chain.

Choosing Future Suppliers to Develop

After you have successfully developed your first supplier, it is up to you how you decide to choose the next supplier to be developed. Still, we strongly suggest that you again carefully consider the ten attributes discussed in Chapter 4. Look at how the supplier impacts your internal inventory levels, how the supplier fits into the true cost model, how they will react to the pull signal system, and how they will respond to your partner development team assisting them in the implementation.

You may choose to develop a supplier that is having quality problems. You may choose to develop a supplier that has a difficult time delivering on time. The key point is that you need to be successful when you develop your first supplier; once your team learns the process of transforming the supplier into a partner, then they will be better prepared to take on other issues, such as quality, on-time delivery, etc.

Input from internal departments is also a key to choosing which suppliers to develop. Throughout this book we've given you a lot of guidance on suppliers, cost, transportation, packaging, etc. The key players outlined in Chapter 3 are valuable assets for the information you need to determine which suppliers would likely make good long-term partners. Try to obtain input from all of these key players, as well as any other department, group, or individuals that may have information relevant to choosing a supplier that would make a good partner.

---

* The glass wall process combines both the information on Lean implementation efforts and daily running of the facility into one area for management to use effectively. It was outlined in the book Harris, C., and R. Harris, **Lean Connections** (Boca Raton, FL: CRC Press, 2008).

Conclusion

In this chapter, we've covered some items that need to be considered when choosing your first supplier to be developed into a partner. This chapter has also led you through a method of developing suppliers into partners by describing a model for improvement.

The model described in this chapter is designed to be a teaching model, in hopes that at the end of the process, partners are able to continually improve on their own without the assistance of outside support. Throughout this process, keep in mind that your goal is long-term, mutually beneficial partnerships.

Chapter 16

The Value Stream Mapping Methodology

Introduction

This chapter details how we have used the value stream mapping methodology to help suppliers implement their Lean enterprise systems. We will do this by identifying the five important components of the methodology for using a value stream map (VSM) to drive Lean enterprise implementation.

This chapter also illustrates how you can use VSMs to identify homework assignments for your supplier partners during your biweekly to monthly visits. The value stream map can play a key role in the implementation of your Lean enterprise system. In this chapter, we'll explain how.

The Value Stream Mapping Methodology

The value stream map is a tool that can drive the implementation of Lean production systems by identifying where improvements need to be made. The VSM provides a common language for Lean practitioners and links material and information flows.

There are five components essential to using the value stream map methodology to implement Lean production systems: product family, the current state value stream map, the future state value stream map, the 30/60/90-day future state value stream map, and, perhaps most important, the comprehensive work plan you'll use to achieve the future state.

The Product Family

It is important to identify how the value stream mapping philosophy can be used and how it cannot. It is very difficult to value stream map a department, but you can value stream map a process *within* a department. For example, it is very difficult to value stream map the human resources department; however, you could use the value stream mapping philosophy to draw a map of the hiring process, and use it to improve the hiring process. The same holds true in a manufacturing facility. It is very difficult to value stream map a production facility, but you can choose a product family and value stream map the production process, from the receiving of raw material to the delivery of finished product to the customer.

So, you choose a product family where your Lean implementation will begin. It's important to choose a *production* product family, not a sales product family. When we choose a product family for Lean implementation, we need to determine that family based upon the production steps that it goes through, not necessarily how it is sold.

Let's say an office furniture company sells a product family based upon the color of the furniture. So they may have a white office furniture line, and they identify all of the products in the white furniture category as a product family. This is perfectly fine from a sales standpoint, but from a production standpoint, we need to look at things a little differently.

Let's assume that the line is made up of a very simple set of office furniture—maybe a chair, a desk, and a filing cabinet. A production product family will not likely be based on the color of the product, but on the production steps that the products go through to be completed. For example, all of the chairs, whether they are white, black, or brown, will go through the same production steps. Therefore, they are likely in the same production product family. The same holds true with the desks and filing cabinets. From a Lean implementation standpoint, we decide on a product family by the production steps a product goes through, rather than how the product may be grouped together and sold.

Figure 16.1 provides a visual representation of how you may determine product families.

As you can see, the chairs go through the same processes, the desks go through the same processes, and the filing cabinets go through their own processes. There are three different product families here, all based on their production process steps: a desk production product family, a chair production product family, and filing cabinet production product family.

	Molding	Stamping	Wheel Assy.	Paint	Wood Finish	Chair Assy.	Cabinet Assy.	Desk Assy.
Black Chair	X		X			X		
White Chair	X		X			X		
Brown Chair	X		X			X		
Black Desk					X			X
Brown Desk					X			X
White Desk					X			X
White Filing Cabinet		X		X			X	
Black Filing Cabinet		X		X			X	
Brown Filing Cabinet		X		X			X	

Figure 16.1   Furniture product family matrix.

Furthermore, when choosing a supplier to develop, you should choose a production product family in that supplier's facility that produces product that is made for your facility. It is true that we are going to be as successful as our supply base, but if we are going to use our resources to assist in their implementation of a Lean enterprise, we want to get the biggest bang for our buck. Therefore, in most cases, a product family that supplies your facility should be chosen for implementation when you enter a supplier for the first time to assist them in the implementation of their Lean enterprise.

The Current State Value Stream Map

Once the product family has been chosen, your next step is to draw the current state value stream map. The current state value stream map is a picture of where the facility is right now as it pertains to the specific product family chosen for improvement. It is important that the map is drawn with information gathered while on the production floor. Over our years of helping facilities implement Lean, we have found that, almost invariably, the people who go to the production floor to draw the value stream maps find that the production floor is not running exactly the way that they had thought it was running.

The information on the value stream map *has* to be correct, because that information will be used to construct the future state map, which will in turn be used to drive implementation efforts. You have probably heard the old saying "garbage in, garbage out." The same adage holds true when dealing with the value stream mapping methodology. Your maps are only going to be as good as the information that is on them. Don't rely on hearsay or what the computer system says *should* be there, but on what you see with your own eyes. Go to the floor and gather the information for yourself so you know that it's correct. Armed with solid information, you can now proceed to drawing your value stream maps.

Let's take a look at a current state value stream map, drawn on the toy truck product family we have been following throughout this book (Figure 16.2).

Looking at this current state value stream map, you can quickly see that the toy truck product family goes through the stamping process, grind process, paint process, and final assembly process before it goes to the shipping department. You can also see that it takes thirty days for the raw material to go first in, first out (FIFO) from the receiving door to the shipping department; this is the production lead time. However, it only takes 296.4 seconds to actually produce a toy truck. Why is it that it takes less than five minutes of assembly or processing time to produce a toy truck, but it takes thirty days for the material to produce that toy truck to get through the process?

The large discrepancy between the processing time and the production lead time means that there's a huge improvement opportunity in this value stream. These discrepancies are usually caused by large inventories throughout the process that cost a lot of money and keep the value stream from performing at full efficiency. These large inventories cause the production lead time to be longer in comparison to the actual product processing time, because the material has to pass through all of the large inventory levels to get through the entire process, which in this case, takes about thirty days. To attack this current state and come up with a plan to improve the value stream, you need to draw a future state value stream map so that everyone involved can understand what the value stream could look like in the future.

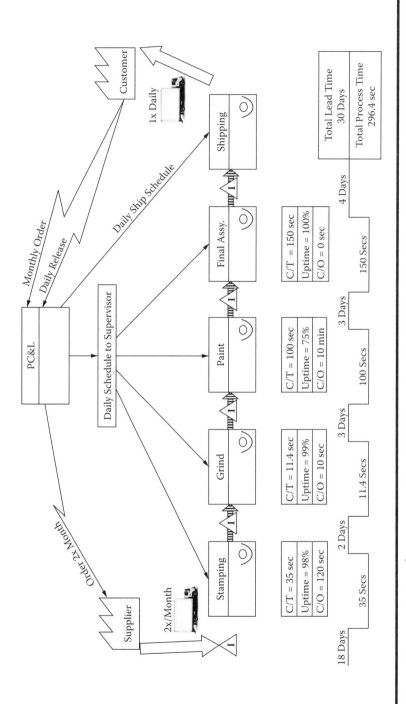

Figure 16.2 Current state value stream map.

The Future State Value Stream Map

The future state value stream map is your game plan for change. It's what you would like the value stream to look like in the future. There are specific questions that you need to answer when drawing a future state map. Our purpose in this book is to develop suppliers into partners, so we won't go into detail describing the eight questions or methods of drawing future state value stream maps (or current state value stream maps). To learn more, pick up one of the books currently on the market that explain the method of drawing current and future state value stream maps in manufacturing processes* and office processes.†

For our purposes, it is imperative to understand how to effectively draw a future state value stream map, because these maps direct improvement ideas and are therefore a key to effective Lean implementation. If you have an improvement idea that does not fit into the future state value stream map, then one of two things is wrong. Either the future state map is incorrect, or the improvement idea isn't worth pursuing. The future state value stream map is where you want to get to in the future, so it should be drawn with that in mind. Figure 16.3 shows a future state value stream map for the toy truck product family.

30/60/90-Day Future State Maps

One of the biggest problems, if not the biggest problem, faced by suppliers who are trying to implement Lean production systems is that they have to continue to run their businesses during implementation. It would be a lot easier to implement Lean production systems if suppliers did not have to worry about delivering product on time to the customer. Obviously, that's not an option, so suppliers have to develop methods that ensure Lean enterprise systems are being implemented at the same time they are running their businesses.

By using the teaching method of implementation discussed in Chapter 15, you can help to ensure Lean implementation in your suppliers' facilities. If your partner development team operates properly, they are leaving the supplier with specific implementation tasks to be accomplished by their next

---

* Rother, M., and J. Shook, **Learning to See** (Cambridge, MA: The Lean Enterprise Institute, 2002).
† Keyte, B., and D. Locher, **The Complete Lean Enterprise** (New York: Productivity Press, 2003).

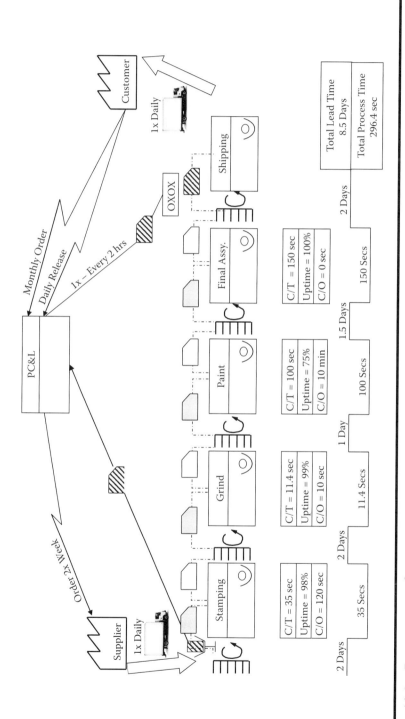

Figure 16.3   Future state value stream map.

visit, either in two weeks or next month. This forces the supplier to take steps toward implementation by the next visit. If they do not accomplish the previous tasks assigned without a good reason, it will quickly become obvious that the supplier is not serious about implementing Lean production systems and may not be a good supplier with whom to form a long-term partnership.

The 30/60/90-day future state value stream maps come into play when choosing the tasks that need to be accomplished. If the partner development team cannot give the supplier the time and guidance needed to apply the necessary pressure for implementation, the 30/60/90-day future state value stream maps can provide pressure to implement if the supplier is serious about implementing. Often, in facilities attempting to implement Lean enterprise systems, employees have their real job and then their Lean implementation job. In this situation, Lean implementation gets pushed to the back burner and sometimes forgotten. There has to be pressure to continue to implement, and creating a thirty-day future state map provides that pressure. Every thirty days, *something* has to be implemented to stay on track. The 30/60/90-day future state methodology applies the needed pressure to keep the implementation moving. This method will also assist the partner development team in choosing what projects should be next.

The first step in this methodology is to draw a thirty-day future state value stream map. This map should have attainable thirty-day goals. Next, a sixty-day future state map should be drawn with attainable sixty-day goals. Finally, a ninety-day future state map should be drawn that includes tasks that can be reasonably accomplished in a ninety-day period.

Every thirty days, the previous thirty-day future state value stream map should become the new current state value stream map. The previous sixty-day map becomes the new thirty-day future state value stream map, and the previous ninety-day future state value stream map becomes the new sixty-day future state value stream map. This means that a new ninety-day future state value stream map needs to be drawn.

This process forces the supplier to do two things that really assist in the implementation of Lean enterprise systems. The first is consistent and ongoing implementation, because the supplier is implementing improvements on a monthly basis that are in line with the future state value stream map. The second is a consistent and ongoing continuous improvement *thought process*, because every ninety days the supplier is drawing a future state map that can be achieved in ninety days.

This type of implementation only works when done with discipline and accountability. Without discipline, the maps may become more like wallpaper than a tool that drives improvement. One way to help with accountability is to have a good, well-designed, comprehensive work plan.

A Comprehensive Work Plan

Unfortunately, while many suppliers can draw the current and future state maps, they fall short of making the changes happen. One of the reasons this happens is the lack of a comprehensive work plan. You need to have a plan in place that details the task, date due, and individual responsible for the task.

In the book *Lean Connections: Making Information Flow Efficiently and Effectively,*[*] we outline the glass wall process, a proven process for quickly and efficiently tracking the Lean implementation efforts in a facility. This same process can hold true when assisting suppliers in their implementation. You need to develop a plan using the value stream mapping methodology; there must be a comprehensive work plan that identifies the task, the due date, and the person responsible for the task; and finally, there must be a system of checks to see if the person that is in charge of completing the project has the necessary assistance to get the task done and is making sufficient progress toward the task.

Many facilities do a good job of identifying the tasks that need to be accomplished, but fall short on the implementation. This often happens because of the lack of follow-up and support given to the person responsible for completing the task. We see it happen this way. Mr. Hudson is given the task of designing, creating, and implementing point-of-use racks at the final assembly area. This task is assigned on March 1 and is scheduled for completion by June 1. Mr. Hudson does not hear from or approach management about this task. The last week of May, he tries to complete the point-of-use delivery racks, but he cannot get it done because he does not have the support he needs to accomplish this task.

This type of story is not uncommon. It happens because Mr. Hudson has his real job and then his Lean implementation. His "real job" takes precedence. He's faced with problem after problem all day long; by the end of the day, he just wants to go home. The Lean implementation efforts continue to get pushed back until it is time for the project to be done.

---

[*] Harris, C., and R. Harris, **Lean Connections Making Information Flow Efficiently and Effectively** (Boca Raton, FL: CRC Press, 2008).

The best way to attack this problem is through cascading audits, or audits that are done by different levels of management at different frequencies cascading upwards.

Mr. Hudson's supervisor should check progress of his assigned task on a weekly basis. The plant or site manager should be checking on progress of value stream implementation on a monthly basis. These audits are not in place to catch someone doing something wrong, but to verify progress and identify where support is needed to complete the tasks.

So, to summarize, there are two major points about comprehensive work plans. The first is that you need one. And second, you need a process to support and verify that the implementation is on schedule and will be completed.

Conclusion

In this chapter, we've explained how to use the value stream mapping methodology to help suppliers implement their Lean enterprise systems by identifying and explaining the five important components of the methodology of utilizing value stream maps to drive Lean enterprise implementation.

This chapter has also shown how the teaching method of biweekly to monthly visits can be planned utilizing the value stream maps as a guide to identify homework projects to assign tasks for improvement. The importance of a detailed comprehensive work plan cannot be emphasized enough. It does not matter how well you plan your improvement ideas and systems; if you cannot execute them, they will not do you any good.

Chapter 17

The Quarterly Review Process

Introduction

This chapter explains a very important event, the quarterly review, which takes place during the development of suppliers into long-term partnerships. Every quarter, the suppliers that have been chosen as good candidates to become partners meet at the customer or a supplier facility.

This method has proven to be a driving factor in the implementation of Lean enterprise systems because it provides information flow, learning opportunities, the sharing of best practices, and creates a little competition. This chapter explains the process of quarterly reviews. We'll also talk about who should attend the quarterly reviews, and why.

The Process

Every quarter, each facility participating in the supplier development program, whether as a supplier or as the customer, needs to meet together at a facility for what we call a quarterly review. Each facility needs to be represented at the review for the review to produce the best results.

Quarterly reviews serve three purposes. The first is so that the management of your facility can observe the progress and understand the importance of the supplier development program. For supplier development to really take off and become ingrained in your organization, you need visibility. The management of your facility has to realize that the development of suppliers is very important to the efficiency of your supply chain. Quarterly reviews act as a constant reminder to management of your supplier development initiative. Furthermore, when the upper management of your facility is present and engaged during the reviews, it sends a message to the suppliers that your leadership is serious and interested in the supplier-partner philosophy.

The second purpose of the quarterly review is to share ideas. A big part of Lean implementation is *understanding* what a Lean enterprise is, but sharing best practices in Lean implementation may be of equal importance. A main theme in this philosophy of supplier development is the long-term partnership mentality. During the quarterly review it is important to realize that everyone is there to get better. The mood of the meeting should be conducive to continuous improvement.

The quarterly review cannot be like a classic supplier meeting. In our mind, classic supplier meetings are much more of a negative experience than a knowledge-sharing one. Classic supplier meetings are based on cost reductions, quality problems, and givebacks. In other words, these meetings are very negative, one sided, and suppliers are always glad when they're over. This quarterly review should in no way resemble those meetings. This meeting must be a positive and productive meeting for everyone involved.

The final purpose of the quarterly review is to create a little competition among partners. As we'll explain in Chapter 18, the quarterly review is set up to encourage competition among the suppliers in terms of the speed and effectiveness with which they are implementing their Lean enterprise systems. A little competition, even if it's not official, can drive suppliers to do more.

Who Should Attend the Quarterly Review?

There are four different categories of attendees at the quarterly review: suppliers' representatives, upper management of your facility, the key players outlined in Chapter 3, and the partner development team.

Let's take a closer look at who exactly should attend the supplier development review, and why they need to be there.

The Supplier

The supplier representatives are very important, since they're going to present their accomplishments from a Lean enterprise implementation standpoint over the past quarter. Because of this, the supplier representative cannot be a salesperson; instead it's best if both the plant manager and his or her head of Lean implementation show up to present their achievements. Try to make it a requirement for the plant manager to present the progress, because it forces the plant managers to be involved in the Lean implementation, and thereby encourages long-term success. This in turn allows the plant managers of the facilities to see and understand the importance of implementing a Lean enterprise system, which in the long term is good for you because the healthier your supply base, the better off you are likely to be.

It is not a bad idea to have the salesperson attend the review even though he or she won't be presenting the Lean enterprise implementation's progress. But he or she needs to be able to understand the partnership that is forming between the customer and the supplier; it's valuable knowledge when dealing with the physical interaction between the supplier and customer, as well as dealing with the purchasing department. For example, the salesperson will hopefully come to understand that offering very large quantities for a small price break is not as appealing as it once was.

Upper Management

The importance of including the upper management of your facility in the quarterly reviews cannot be overstated. They are really there to observe, but their presence speaks volumes to a supply base that may be wondering how long this initiative will actually last, or whether it's simply the flavor of the month or initiative of the quarter. Additionally, it is important for management to see how the process works and how it benefits the company. You need the support of upper management to get this done, and the best way to cultivate and keep the support of upper management is to continually illustrate the importance of developing the supply base.

The quarterly review normally takes two days, but you will only need upper management there on the second day (we'll talk more about this in Chapter 18). So, you will only have to request one day per quarter for your upper management to devote to supplier development.

The Key Players

The third group that should be present at the quarterly review is the key player group identified in Chapter 3. Each key player has a specific reason to be in the quarterly review. The internal continuous improvement team is there to present further ideas for improvement in the suppliers' value streams and for the sharing of best practices. Your internal continuous improvement team should always be looking for ways to improve your own internal Lean enterprise systems, and this is a great opportunity for them to sit down and see what others are doing to implement Lean enterprise systems.

The purchasing department will likely know the history of the relationship between you and the supplier, and more important, they need to have a firm understanding of what a Lean enterprise looks like and what is being done to accomplish the goal. When companies don't involve purchasing in the process, purchasing continues their function as they always have, even though it may be detrimental to the development of your new Lean enterprise system. Our hope is that by having them at the quarterly review along with upper management, many current measures (i.e., piece price cost) will be addressed, and new measurements, such as total cost to the value stream, will be discussed. Purchasing will no doubt play a large role in the long-term development of the supply base, so it is very important that they are part of the process.

Material control is another important part of any Lean implementation. Material flow, whether components in a production facility or papers in an office, is very important in a Lean implementation. If you have been successfully implementing Lean initiatives in your facility, then you likely see the value and importance of a solid and capable material control organization, which controls the schedule and material flow in a facility. They need to be part of the quarterly review to see what is taking place and provide input on how the suppliers can better support the customer. The supplier can also openly communicate with the material control organization in this process and can relay to them what they can do to allow the suppliers to more efficiently support the customer. A solid representative from material control is a must at the quarterly review.

Product engineering is next on the list because they are important for the future. There are not very many research and development individuals at the Lean implementation meetings that we attend, and this poses a big problem for the future state, since the research and development department is likely designing what will be produced in the upcoming years. If they possess limited to no Lean knowledge, you can't expect them to design product with a Lean production process in mind. They need to be included in Lean enterprise implementation, especially the supplier development quarterly reviews.

The research and design department needs to understand not only the process of Lean implementation, but also the capabilities and offerings of the supply base. Too many times, a product is designed without a lot of thought given to how you will supply components and who is going to produce the product. In other instances, the components in the product are overengineered, while there were stock components from a current supplier that could easily be substituted. Our goal in having the research and development people at the quarterly review is to familiarize them with both the Lean supplier development initiative and the suppliers themselves.

Next up is quality. The quarterly supplier development reviews provide a good opportunity for the quality department to cover any current or potential quality problems and for the supplier to talk to the quality department. Any quality problem disrupts the flow of value, and every time the flow is disrupted, it costs the company money in the form of time, production problems, etc. Poor quality cannot be accepted from your supplier partner. Quality should therefore be present at these quarterly reviews to address any quality problems and work with the suppliers to resolve any issues.

Transportation is the last of the key players. Without components, the facility will not run, so the organization or individual in charge of component transportation needs to attend the supplier development quarterly review. This will once again provide two-way communication, where transportation and the suppliers can discuss any problems and ways to improve.

The Partner Development Team

The partner development team runs the supplier development quarterly review. All members of the partner development team should be present on both days of the review. Since this is their job, time shouldn't be a factor, as it is with upper management and the key players, who will only be needed on the second day.

The partner development team must ensure that the review stays as close to on time as possible, and that the format (described in Chapter 18) is followed. Finally, and most important, it is the responsibility of the partner development team to set the tone of the meeting.

If this review turns into a classic supplier meeting in which the customer beats up on the supplier for eight hours, the entire supplier development program will suffer great harm. It will most likely destroy any progress that you have made, make future progress very difficult, and diminish the value of the quarterly review. However, if the quarterly review is conducted in such a way that partners can truly work together and benefit from the sharing of ideas, it is hard to overestimate its value.

Conclusion

By now, you should have an understanding of the methodology of quarterly reviews, who should attend, and why those individuals or departments should attend.

In the next chapter, we'll explain the agenda for the two-day supplier development quarterly review, giving you a better view of the reason each attendee is there, and showing you a way to use your quarterly reviews to effectively develop your chosen suppliers into long-term, mutually beneficial relationships.

Chapter 18

Supplier Development Quarterly Review Agenda

Introduction

This chapter illustrates an agenda for a successful two-day quarterly review. Each of the days is different: the first day is a teaching day; the second day is a presentation day.

This chapter explains how to effectively set up an agenda for the quarterly review and provides sample agendas. You need well-defined agendas for the quarterly reviews, and it's important to standardize the reviews as much as possible so that the suppliers can get comfortable with the process. We want to be sure that quarterly reviews are beneficial for everyone involved.

Location of Meeting

The meeting location can vary. The first quarterly review should probably occur at your facility, since you're leading the initiative. After the first meeting, we encourage you to conduct the next quarterly review at a partner facility.

Why hold a quarterly review meeting at a partner facility? There are multiple reasons, including encouraging networking and partnerships within your supply base, but the primary reason is for sharing best practices among facilities. Unless you believe that all of the best practices are available at your facility, you likely can see the benefit of seeing other facilities.

Furthermore, if you can coordinate the day 1 topic (covered in the next section) to the facility that is hosting the review, it can open the door to some very good learning opportunities. For example, if the topic covered in day 1 is standardized work, then it would be nice to have a supplier that is exceptional with standardized work host the quarterly review so that the participants can go to the floor and see standardized work in action.

Day 1: Continuous Knowledge Improvement and Networking

The first day of the quarterly review is set up to be more of a day of learning and networking than a day of evaluation. For day 1, the partner development team chooses a topic that they believe would be best for the suppliers to learn, and teach on that topic. Day 1 also provides a more laid back atmosphere for the suppliers to get to know each other. Once again, if you are developing a partnership mentality, everyone has the same goal—success—and may be more likely to share and propose new ways to improve their processes in an informal environment.

Setting up day 1 in this way allows the partner development team to control the content taught to the suppliers and ensure that all suppliers are hearing the same thing. Also, the partner development team can use its field experience to gauge the need for training and plan accordingly.

As you can see in the agenda in Figure 18.1, the last item for the day is a facility tour. The first quarterly review at your facility will probably be a good one, because the suppliers will get to the production floor to see how their components are used. This may not seem like an original idea, but although the supplier sales personnel may go to the floor to see how the product they sell is used, the suppliers' production managers may have not had that opportunity. This proves to be a good exercise because when a supplier sees how their component is handled and used in a facility, this can foster some improvement ideas for the future.

When the quarterly review is hosted by a supplier, the plant tour is a little different. The main goal in this case is the sharing of best practices. As discussed previously, if the partner development team chooses a facility that excels at the topic, such as standardized work, being addressed in the training, it can be more than a sharing of best practices. This can provide an excellent learning opportunity for the participants both in the classroom and on the production floor.

Your partner development team will likely have the best handle on the Lean enterprise implementation material, and should lead the first day of the training. Be sure to align the topic of the day and the partner development team member's specialty; for example, if the partner development team member is the value stream mapping specialist, he or she should teach on the topic of value stream mapping. Training needs to be conducted with solid material and a knowledgeable trainer. A list of possible training courses to begin the first few quarterly reviews could be:

- Workplace organization (may be best for first review)
- Continuous flow*
- Material flow†
- Information flow‡
- Developing a Lean workforce§
- Standardized work

This is not an all-inclusive list, but it can give you some ideas as to future training sessions. If you are walking all of your suppliers down a similar path of implementation, try to follow that path with your training topics. Figure 18.1 is a sample agenda for the first day.

Day 2: Review of Progress

The second day of the quarterly review is more goals oriented. During day 2, you'll check the progress of Lean implementation and partner development. As you will see in day 2's sample agenda (Figures 18.2 and 18.3), it begins with a welcome, but quickly goes into presentations by the suppliers that are attending the review.

---

* Rother, M., and R. Harris, **Creating Continuous Flow** (Cambridge, MA: Lean Enterprise Institute, 2001).
† Harris, R., C. Harris, and E. Wilson, **Making Materials Flow** (Cambridge, MA: Lean Enterprise Institute, 2003).
‡ Harris, C., and R. Harris, **Lean Connections** (Boca Raton, FL: CRC Press, 2008).
§ Harris, C., and R. Harris, **Developing a Lean Workforce** (New York: Productivity Press, 2007).

SAMPLE AGENDA
Day 1 Agenda – Quarterly Review

7:30	a.m.	–	8:00	a.m.	Coffee and Registration	All
8:00	a.m.	–	8:10	a.m.	Opening Remarks	PDT-Leader
8:10	a.m.	–	9:15	a.m.	Workplace Organization	Instructor
9:15	a.m.	–	9:30	a.m.	Break	All
9:30	a.m.	–	11:00	a.m.	Workplace Organization	Instructor
11:00	a.m.	–	11:15	a.m.	Break	All
11:15	a.m.	–	12:00	noon	Workplace Organization	Instructor
12:00	noon	–	1:00	p.m.	Lunch	All
1:00	p.m.	–	2:30	p.m.	Workplace Organization	Instructor
2:30	p.m.	–	2:45	p.m.	Break	All
2:45	p.m.	–	5:00	p.m.	Facility Tour	Plant Manager
5:00	p.m.				Meeting Concludes	All
6:00	p.m.	–	10:00	p.m.	Possible Dinner for Suppliers	

PDT-Leader = Partner Development Team Leader

Figure 18.1   Day 1 agenda.

The first quarterly review will be an interesting experience for you and your suppliers. You will likely have some suppliers that show up with excellent presentations and implementation results, as well as some suppliers that do not have very good material. In other words, at the first quarterly review you will likely have some suppliers that have taken things very seriously and other suppliers that do not take the meeting as seriously. It will probably be evident which suppliers are serious and which are not.

The format of the presentations will also likely be very different, and that's okay. You will probably have not gotten everyone up to the same level of implementation, because you have not had time to give each supplier an equal amount of time from the partner development team. Therefore, the suppliers will be at different levels of implementation.

You may have some suppliers show what they have done on workplace organization. You may have some say that they have just begun and that it is their first experience with the Lean philosophy. Whatever happens during this first quarterly review, keep the meeting positive and helpful.

The second quarterly review will be different. There is a strict format that the presentations should follow from the second quarterly review on,

SAMPLE AGENDA (1st Visit)
Day 2 Agenda – Quarterly Review

7:30	a.m.	–	8:00	a.m.	Coffee and Registration	All
8:00	a.m.	–	8:10	a.m.	Opening Remarks	Head Person
8:10	a.m.	–	9:40	a.m.	3 Supplier Presentations	Suppliers
9:40	a.m.	–	10:00	a.m.	Break	All
10:00	a.m.	–	12:00	noon	4 Supplier Presentations	Suppliers
12:00	noon	–	1:00	p.m.	Lunch	All
1:00	p.m.	–	2:30	p.m.	3 Supplier Presentations	Suppliers
2:30	p.m.	–	2:45	p.m.	Break	All
2:45	p.m.	–	4:15	p.m.	3 Supplier Presentations	Suppliers
4:15	p.m.	–	4:45	p.m.	Presentation Format for 2nd Review PDT-Leader
4:45	p.m.	–	5:00	p.m.	Closing Remarks	Plant Manager

PDT-Leader = Partner Development Team Leader

Figure 18.2 **Sample agenda for quarterly reviews.**

SAMPLE AGENDA (Future Visits)
Day 2 Agenda – Quarterly Review

7:30	a.m.	–	8:00	a.m.	Coffee and Registration	All
8:00	a.m.	–	8:10	a.m.	Opening Remarks	Head Person
8:10	a.m.	–	9:40	a.m.	3 Supplier Presentations	Suppliers
9:40	a.m.	–	10:00	a.m.	Break	All
10:00	a.m.	–	12:00	noon	4 Supplier Presentations	Suppliers
12:00	noon	–	1:00	p.m.	Lunch	All
1:00	p.m.	–	2:30	p.m.	3 Supplier Presentations	Suppliers
2:30	p.m.	–	2:45	p.m.	Break	All
2:45	p.m.	–	4:15	p.m.	3 Supplier Presentations	Suppliers
4:15	p.m.	–	4:45	p.m.	Next Review Details	PDT-Leader
4:45	p.m.	–	5:00	p.m.	Closing Remarks	PDT-Leader

PDT-Leader = Partner Development Team Leader

Figure 18.3 **Sample agenda for quarterly reviews.**

focusing on current state value stream map (VSM), future state VSM, work (implementation) plan, accomplishments to date, and savings. For this reason, it is probably best to conduct the value stream mapping training before or during the first quarterly review. Appendix B illustrates a possible short presentation for quarterly reviews. The previous figure shows what the agenda might be for the second day of the first and future quarterly reviews.

Depending on how you begin the implementation at the supplier, you have likely started with either the eight wastes of production, workplace organization, value stream maps, or some combination of those. It is very important, if your format for the second day of the quarterly review is based on the value stream mapping methodology, that you spend sufficient time covering value stream mapping in a way that is well thought out and well delivered. It is important to remember that the value stream maps are the central tool for the implementation of Lean enterprise systems.

Additional Notes on Quarterly Reviews

A few notes about the second day of the quarterly reviews. The first is that it is not designed to make people or suppliers look bad, although it could quickly turn into that if not managed properly. Therefore, questions throughout the process should be limited to the partner development team through the presentation, and then opened up to the rest of the people in the room. If a derogatory or unproductive comment or question comes up, it needs to be addressed *immediately* by the partner development team. This meeting cannot turn into a negative experience or you will risk losing any positive outcomes from the quarterly review.

The second point we want to make is that there will likely be a competition during this process. Suppliers don't like being outperformed by other suppliers. Particularly after the first quarterly review, when the suppliers see how the process goes, do not be surprised if you begin to see some outstanding results. Additionally, you will discover which suppliers are serious about the process and which are not.

The final note is that if used properly, the quarterly review process can be *the driver* for continuous improvement within the supply base. The quarterly reviews provide a way to monitor progress, share best practices, and network for improvement. They also allow the facility to see how the supplier development initiative is going and create positive competition between suppliers to continually get better.

Conclusion

Remember, each day of a successful quarterly review is different. The first day of the supplier development quarterly review is a teaching day dedicated to topics that the partner development team determines the supply base needs. The second day is for sharing, where the progress of the supplier development initiative can be monitored.

This chapter has attempted to explain how to effectively set up an agenda for the quarterly review. When used properly, the quarterly review process has proven to be an outstanding resource for driving the Lean implementation in an organization.

Afterword

Our goal for this book was to provide you with a methodology for dealing with and developing suppliers—a methodology that's different from the classic cost-only model of sourcing. The future holds a different type of competition than we've seen in the past, a comprehensive competition where it's not your facility versus your competitor's facility, but your supply chain versus their supply chain.

The supply base is a big part of the supply chain, and developing that supply base into a true asset to the overall flow of value is an important part of making any supply chain a global player. By now, you've learned the benefits of our philosophy and how to choose the players who will ensure your long-term success. We've discussed the importance of internal operations, the vital role of the Plan for Every Part (PFEP), how to appropriately size your inventory, the true cost model, the importance of linkages with your suppliers, and provided a program to develop your suppliers into long-term partners in a Lean supply chain.

It's a lot of information. Now, it's time for you to take this information and use it to develop your suppliers into true partners, and help them implement Lean enterprise systems in their facilities. If your supply partners can create true Lean enterprise systems where continuous improvement is a constant in their facilities, it will benefit their facility, their employees, your facility, your employees, and your customer—the entire supply chain.

Thank you for taking the time to read this book. We hope that you've found it helpful. Remember, always think ahead to your next improvement.

Best wishes on your Lean journey.

Appendix A: The Eight Wastes and Their Relationship to Supplier Development

Introduction

The eight forms of waste are an excellent way to point out inefficiencies in a system; they can really get thought processes moving and spur continuous improvement ideas.

In this appendix, we take a look at the classic seven forms of waste and relate them to material flow, and explain an eighth form of waste that's prevalent in most organizations: the waste of knowledge.

The Importance of Material Flow

It does not matter how good a facility's production operations are: if operations does not have any material, producing product is impossible. Therefore, Lean enterprise implementation focuses on material, which is imperative to efficient operations.

The first subject taught in Lean Enterprise 101 is likely the eight forms of waste* (see Figure A.1). On the surface it may not look like the eight forms of waste deal directly with material flow, but they all do. In Figure A.1, you can see that the wastes are in the dandelion and the causes are at the roots.

---

* The first seven forms of waste are taken from Ohno, T., **Toyota Production System: Beyond Large-Scale Production** (Portland, OR: Productivity Press, 1998), 19–20.

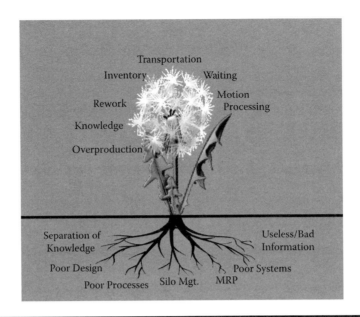

Figure A.1   Dandelion of waste.

Each form of waste is not the *specific* problem, but a symptom of a bigger problem that deserves our attention. Each of the eight forms of waste is directly related to material flow, and it's important at this point to examine them and how they relate to supplier development.

Waste 1: Overproduction

Overproduction is the most significant form of waste, because it provides the environment for all of the other forms of waste that can exist in the system. Overproduction can also cause a number of problems in your relationship with your suppliers.

Overproduction can take two forms, either making product faster than is required by the customer or making more than the customer requires. This form of waste can be detrimental to your suppliers and your Lean supply chain as a whole. When you say that you are going to make a certain quantity of product, your supply chain expects for you to make a certain quantity of parts. If your organization makes the quantity of parts that it has planned, then you can rest assured that your suppliers are also making what will be needed. However, if your organization does not make what it was supposed to make when it was supposed to make it, your suppliers are forced to guess the quantity that you are going to make. This leads to higher inventory levels, longer lead times, and higher costs for everyone involved.

Waste 2: Waste of Making Defective Products (Rework)

Rework, sometimes called correction, is when a product or task was not produced correctly the first time and someone must return to the task and fix the defect. Defects happen not only on the production floor, but in office processes as well. The waste of rework is a good example to show that the eight forms of waste are a symptom of a bigger problem. Whenever you have a defective product or task that needs to be corrected, the problem is not the correction, but the process that caused the need for the correction.

As we've reiterated throughout this book, the quality of the product a supplier produces for you is very important. In the classic model of sourcing product based on piece price cost, quality may not be considered as much as it should, but as you now know, the cost of poor quality can be significant. Many facilities inspect product received from suppliers checking for defective parts. This is a cost (see true cost, Section 3) and inconvenience that you and your organization should not be forced to accept.

Anytime there is a quality problem it disrupts the flow of value to the customer. Whenever the flow of value to the customer is disrupted, it cost the company time and money.

Waste 3: Waste of Time on Hand (Waiting)

The flow (or lack of flow) of material sometimes causes waiting in the value stream. If at any point in the production or flow of value from the customer, someone in the system has to wait, there is a problem. Waiting for material, information, or people is a cost that needs to be addressed. If material does not arrive at the facility on time, the disruption to the value stream can be great. When production waits on material, they must decide whether to continue to wait (waste) or to change over to run another product that hadn't been scheduled to run in that time slot; this can potentially lead to the waste of overproduction. Whether production chooses to continue to wait or change over, each decision is less than optimal for the continual flow of value to the customer. Waiting leads to a cost that we should attempt to eliminate, through choosing reliable suppliers with reliable delivery methods, among other attributes.

Waste 4: Processing

Processing waste occurs when you do something for the customer that they do not require. Many times this happens because of the training methods and process control in the organization. Take, for example, a purchasing agent who was trained by the previous purchasing agent in a facility, who of course was trained by the previous purchasing agent. In other words, the purchasing department has been trained by generation-to-generation knowledge. The current purchasing agent is the third generation to be trained the same way. On the surface, this may sound like a positive point, but this situation also means that there are only three individuals who know how to properly do the job, and two of them are not there anymore.

When organizations train their employees this way, without a well-documented standardized work process (i.e., process control), employees may wind up doing work that is not required by the customer. Let's say that the same purchasing agent gets a shipping notification electronically, and uses it to verify that the shipment is correct. The purchasing agent also receives a paper copy of the shipping notification and files it because the first purchasing agent (three generations previous) requested the notification because he or she did not have an electronic system. The supplier was never told that the electronic system was all that was needed, and so it has continued to send the shipping notification via overnight mail. This is a waste of processing, in part because there was never any documented standardized work to refer to, to see if the paper copy of the shipping notice was needed.

At this point, you're probably thinking that this is the supplier's fault, and that it does not impact your organization if they choose to consistently perform wastefully. You may be right, but if you want to create a supply chain that can compete in the global economy, you should eliminate *all* waste, in the *entire* value stream to reduce the total cost to the customer. Remember, you're only as healthy as your supply base.

Waste 5: Waste of Movement (Inefficient Machine and Operator Motion)

Any movement of machines or operators that does not support the just-in-time mentality is waste. The goal in a Lean supply chain is to eliminate any wasted movement.

What movement in your supply chain does not add value to the product? Do you have multiple data inputs? What is the process of receiving material into the system? Are there any movements in this process that are pure waste that we could eliminate?

Waste 6: Waste of Transportation (Inefficient Transportation of Material)

Do you or a department in your organization move material in a way that is not efficient? Do you have a staging area? Is material moved multiple times before it is used? Do you do more with material than is required to complete the value-added product?

Material movement can be very costly. Material should flow from the dock to the purchased parts supermarket, from the purchased parts supermarket to the fingertips of the value-added operator, then to a work-in-process (WIP) market, finished goods market, or the final customer. The material should not stop unless those stops are planned and important to the efficiency of the overall operating system. The movement of material is where money is made, so it should certainly be a focus of any operating system, not only production, but also office processes.

Waste 7: Waste of Inventory

Inventory costs organizations a great deal of money, because of the labor it takes to deal with the inventory, the space that the inventory takes up on the production floor, and the cash that it eats up because the inventory has been paid for, but is not currently being used to produce a value-added product.

Inventory is waste, albeit sometimes necessary. Let's take a look at Figure A.2. Process A runs 80% uptime* and process B runs 80% uptime. If process A were coupled with process B, meaning that process A runs directly into process B, then the two processes would run less than the 80% uptime because when process A breaks down, so will process B, and when process B breaks down, so will process A. So, in the figure, there is a first-in, first-

---

* Uptime is the percentage of time that a machine actually runs, compared to what it was scheduled to run.

Figure A.2

out (FIFO) lane that holds inventory. The reason for this inventory is to have a higher uptime. By having this inventory in the system, both process A and process B can run at 80% uptime, because when process B breaks down, process A can continue to build and fill the FIFO lane. And vice versa, when process A breaks down, process B can continue to run by pulling product out of the FIFO lane. In a Lean environment, inventory is in the forefront. Large inventory levels can cover up a lot of problems in an organization; an organization with a large inventory to fall back on may not be compelled to be as efficient as it should be.

Almost every Lean enterprise initiative deals with material movement in some way, either directly or indirectly. Inventory is material. Therefore, the movement and reduction of inventory should be a focus in an environment implementing Lean enterprise.

Waste 8: Knowledge

As we have helped people throughout the world implement robust Lean enterprise systems focused on material movement, we have noticed an eighth waste: the waste of knowledge. Many times, knowledge is kept in pockets in our organizations. For example, purchasing information is kept only in purchasing, design information in design, and so on. In an organization implementing Lean enterprise systems, the goal is not only to implement systems, but also to disseminate the knowledge.

When dealing with the waste of knowledge it is important to try to get to a position where knowledge is freely shared between people and departments. Currently, in many companies, knowledge is seen as power and is only released on a need-to-know basis. This can greatly inhibit implementation and continuous improvement in any organization, whether it is implementing Lean enterprise or not.

Appendix B: Sample Standard Supplier Quarterly Review Presentation

PCB Limited

Quarterly Review Presentation

Figure B.1

Agenda

- Current State Value Stream Map
- Future State Value Stream Map
- Implementation Plan
- Accomplishments and Savings

Figure B.2

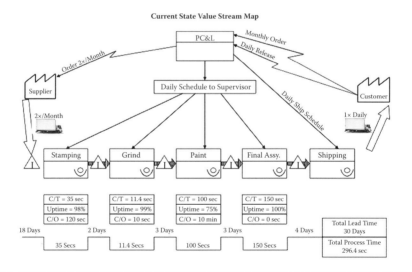

Current State Value Stream Map

Figure B.3

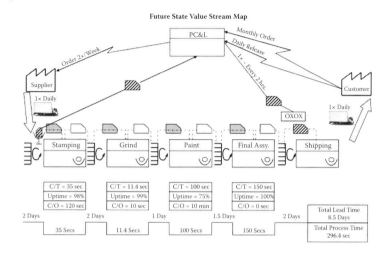

Figure B.4

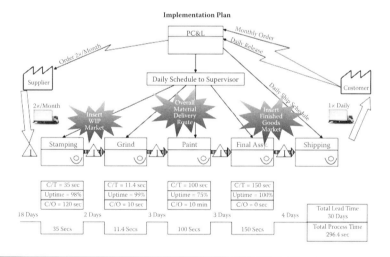

Figure B.5

Implementation Plan

- JT Burnette to size WIP market by 6-1-10. Implement 6-17-10.

- CJ to develop material delivery route with team and implement first route stop 6-17-10.

- R. A. Harris to implement finished goods market sized to customer demand on 6-17-10.

Figure B.6   Implementation Plan Slide with Kaizen Bursts

Accomplishments and Savings

- % Improvement in Inventory Reductions
- % Improvement in Floor Space Reduction
- % Improvement in Lead-Time Reduction
- % Improvement in Productivity
- % Improvement in Quality
- % Improvement in On-Time Delivery

Figure B.7

Next Steps

- We plan to complete the current implementation plan by the next quarterly review.
- We plan to have a new implementation plan, with new objectives by the next quarterly review.

Figure B.8

Index

A

Advisory team, role of key players in supplier development, 25
After-use costs, returnable containers, 130
Agendas
    partner development team visits, 139, 140, 141
    quarterly review, 161–167
Attitude, criteria for choosing suppliers, 28
Average daily usage (ADU), sizing number of pull signals, 111–112

B

Bradshaw, Herb, 3–9
Buffer
    purchased parts (PPB), 113
    supermarket, 48–50
Bus route development, xvi–xvii

C

Capacity, choosing suppliers, 28–29
Capital cost, sourcing model inputs, 92
Cardboard boxes, 129–130
Carrying costs, total inventory cost, 79, 80
Cash flow, benefits of partnership strategy, 7
Change costs, 65–72
    definitions
        inspection cost, 67–68
        inventory cost, 71–72
        lost time cost, 66
        print change cost, 69–70
        testing cost, 69
        tooling cost and amortization, 71

travel costs, 66
    sourcing model inputs, 92–95
        inspection and testing, 94
        inventory, 95
        print changes, 94
        tooling and tooling amortization, 94–95
        travel and lost time cost, 92, 94
Choosing supplier for long-term partnership, 27–32
    attributes of suppliers, 27–32
        attitude, 28
        capacity, 28–29
        credit standing, 30–31
        flexibility to package, 31–32
        on-time delivery, 29–30
        payment terms (pay on pull), 30
        quality level, 28
        true cost model standing, 32
        vital expertise, 29
        volume commodity, 31
    decision makers, 27
Communications
    importance of, 19
    of key players in supplier development, 17–19
    pull signals; See Pull signals/systems
Competitive advantage, supply chain and, 16
Comprehensive work plan, value stream mapping methodology, 153–154
Consignment, ongoing cost, 76–77
Containers
    decision making by supplier, 38–39; See also Packaging/shipping
    supplier-partner approach, 15